BLACKSMITH'S CRAFT

FOX CHAPEL
PUBLISHING

THE BLACKSMITH'S CRAFT

The BLACKSMITH'S CRAFT

an introduction to Smithing for apprentices

and craftsmen

Published by

COUNCIL FOR SMALL INDUSTRIES
IN RURAL AREAS

Dear Reader:

We're very happy to bring the classic *Blacksamithing Series* from COSIRA (Council for Small Industries in Rural Areas) back into print. In the 35 years I have worked as a bookseller and publisher, certain iconic titles stick out. This series is one of those considered a classic because the photographs, text, and illustrations are so complete and highly focused on its subject.

The series:
- *Blacksmith's Craft* (978-1-4971-0046-6)
- *Wrought Ironwork* (978-1-4971-0064-0)
- *Decorative Ironwork* (978-1-4971-0063-3)

You hold the *Blacksmith's Craft* volume in your hand. As you read, please be aware that we have not made any attempt to update the techniques or tools. Consider this treasure trove of knowledge a time capsule from the past.

May you be inspired to pick up the blacksmith's hammer and try your hand at this ancient skill.

Enjoy!

Alan Giagnocavo, Publisher
Fox Chapel Publishing

ISBN 978-1-4971-0046-6

The Cataloging-in-Publication Data is on file with the Library of Congress

To learn more about the other great books from Fox Chapel Publishing, or to find a retailer near you, call toll-free 800-457-9112 or visit us at *www.FoxChapelPublishing.com*.

We are always looking for talented authors. To submit an idea, please send a brief inquiry to acquisitions@foxchapelpublishing.com.

Printed in China
First printing

Contents

v

PART IV

Illustrations

PART I

Note.—The line drawings and half-tone illustrations *in the Lessons* in Parts II, III and IV are not included in this list.

PREFACE

This book has been published by the Council for Small Industries in Rural Areas because there appeared to be no text book on blacksmithing today which could meet the needs of craftsmen, technical schools and apprentices' training centres. The lack of such a book was a handicap to the teaching of this subject and particularly to young men who are receiving instruction from the Council in country workshops. Although written primarily for these men, it will also be of great value to many other craftsmen and apprentices whose work depends on a sound knowledge of the behaviour of iron and steel.

The skill of the smith has been faithfully recorded in sequences of still photographs married to brief descriptive captions. The sequences are arranged in lessons which should not be difficult to follow if text, drawings and photographs are carefully studied. The Council realizes that some of the methods shown and described are not the only ones possible. In such cases the variations have been carefully considered, and the methods chosen have been those which seemed best for the beginner: as he gains experience, the smith can develop his own variations of a technique.

The Smith also sitting by the anvil,
And considering the iron work,
The vapour of the fire wasteth his flesh,
And he fighteth with the heat of the furnace;
The noise of the hammer and the anvil is ever in his ears,
And his eyes look still upon the pattern of the thing that he maketh;
He setteth his mind to finish his work,
And watcheth to polish it perfectly:

Ecclesiasticus

INTRODUCTION

FORGING is the oldest method of making things from iron and steel. It remains an essential craft, because farmers still need within easy reach of their farms workshops where they can be sure of an efficient and prompt repair service. To give such a service today, the skill of a blacksmith must be combined with the techniques of gas or arc welding and flame cutting, but the craftsman who possesses only the techniques of a welder without a knowledge of forging will be seriously handicapped. His lack of smithing skill will oblige him to use welding and flame cutting for jobs which could be done cheaper and better by forging.

An example is the fitting illustrated in Fig. 1. A welder could easily cut the plate and two gussets with a gas cutter from any scrap available, but he is unlikely to have a suitable piece of tube. Without a knowledge of smithing, the only way to make the tube would be to drill and bore a solid piece of shaft, a slow and expensive job. The blacksmith made the tube in Fig. 1 by rolling a piece of plate round a mandrel and then welding the seam, thus saving time and material.

Metal forged at the correct heat loses none of its strength but if, for instance, a piece of metal is merely heated by a blow pipe flame and

Fig. 1

pulled or hammered over a vice, its structure is weakened and may give under strain. A blacksmith working hot metal on the anvil comes to understand his material better than he could in any other way. This is especially true of the smith who turns to ornamental ironwork in his spare moments, for this, besides being to many smiths an absorbing creative art and relief from their heavy work, is an excellent way of discovering the characteristic behaviour of iron. For these reasons, a blacksmith who also has a knowledge of welding techniques can give the farmer a much more versatile and useful service than the man who cannot forge his metal.

The basis of the blacksmith's craft is set out in the pages which follow. There are four parts. Part I describes the smith's simple equipment and his tools, his fuel and his fire, the processes he uses in his work and his raw materials. Parts II, III and IV open with a description of a particular technique which is essential to the lessons which are set out step by step in each part. Each of the photographs by which a technique is illustrated shows some detail of particular technical significance such as the position of the body, the correct grip of the tool in the hand, the angle at which the work is held. At the head of each lesson is a line drawing of the piece to be made, so that the progressive stages of the exercise will be more readily understood, and the relation of drawings to solid objects will become familiar.

A smith who has mastered these thirty-seven lessons will know the essentials of his craft.

PART 1

CHAPTER 1

THE BLACKSMITH'S EQUIPMENT

Forge equipment consists of the Hearth, the Blast, the Anvil and the Bench and Vice.

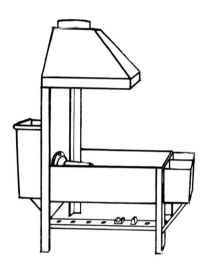

Fig. 2

THE HEARTH

As cast iron is resistant to corrosion it is an ideal material for a hearth in constant use, but where the work is intermittent, a hearth made of mild steel plate is satisfactory. The Council for Small Industries in Rural Areas can supply drawings of a steel hearth (Fig. 2) which is simple to make, either by riveting or arc welding. It is important that the hearth should be well proportioned to allow the fire to form its own bed amongst the burned cinders and ashes. In addition to the place for the fire, a water trough and a container for fuel are needed. The most convenient arrangement is shown in Fig. 2, where the water and fuel troughs are made in one piece and fitted to the front of the hearth.

1

THE BLAST

An important feature of the hearth is the Blast Pipe, called the *tuyere* or *tue iron*. The most efficient tuyere is water cooled (A in Fig. 3) so that it

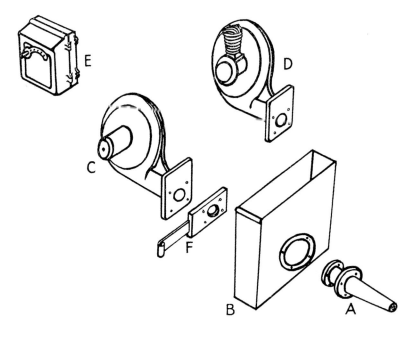

Fig. 3

can stick well out into the fire without the nose getting burned. In a well designed hearth, the tuyere passes through a cast-iron backplate which is detachable. The cooling water which circulates through the tuyere is contained in an open-topped tank just behind the hearth or, if space is short, it can be piped to a tank in a convenient position. The tank should have a lid to keep out dirt and reduce evaporation; it is wise to use rain water to avoid scaling up the inside of the tuyere. For general repair work a tuyere 16″ long with a $\frac{3}{4}$″ air hole is suitable. It is set horizontally on the centre line of the hearth-back with the hole 3″ below the level of the top of the side plates.

The blast is produced by either a bellows or a hand- or power-driven blower. The electrically driven blower (C in Fig. 3) is by far the most convenient, and a size suitable for the average hearth will consume less than a unit of electricity per day. The normal size will blow a second fire for occasional jobs. If electricity is not available, the same type of blower fitted with a petrol engine (D in Fig. 3) can be obtained. One type of set, driven by petrol engine, is fitted with a dynamotor and battery which makes it self-starting, and also provides 12-volt lighting for the shop. Although it may be possible to vary the speed of an electrically driven blower by a regulator (E in Fig. 3) or an engine driven set by the throttle, a valve is essential for accurate control of the blast. This may be a sliding shutter (F in Fig. 3), a butterfly valve, or an ordinary full-way rotating plug-cock. Whatever type is used, the control should work perfectly smoothly and be within easy reach of the blacksmith's free hand.

THE ANVIL

A good quality anvil is made of wrought iron or steel with a hardened steel top and is well worth the extra cost. Working on a bad anvil is like jumping on a heap of sand, whereas working on a good anvil set on a proper foundation is like jumping on a springboard—the rebound from one blow helps towards the next. Anvil patterns may vary for different purposes, but for general work it should have a long and finely tapered bick as shown in Fig. 4 which is a 'London Pattern' anvil standing on a welded angle steel

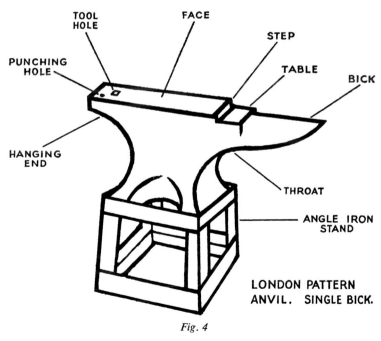

Fig. 4

3

stand. Although the face or top of the anvil is hardened, the bick and table, which is the square part between the bick and the face, are usually left soft. When cutting off with a chisel, the work should always be moved to the table before the final blow to avoid damaging the chisel edge. On a new anvil the front and back edges of the face are left sharp and it is advisable to round these off carefully with a carborundum file or a portable grinder in the places shown in Fig. 5. There are two holes in the face of an anvil; the square or hardy hole and the round or punching hole. It is a good plan to chamfer the edges of the square hole so that the hardy sits tight to the anvil face; this is also a convenience when using the hole for setting slightly curved bars. The liveliness or spring of an anvil is much improved by mounting it on a wooden block, preferably made from a squared-up trunk of elm. This should be sunk at least 3′ into the ground with the grain standing vertically. The disadvantage of setting up an anvil like this in the modern agricultural engineering shop is that the block cannot be moved out of the way. It may be more convenient to have a fabricated steel or cast-iron stand but, where space permits, it is a distinct advantage to have a wooden block.

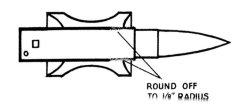

ROUND OFF
TO 1/8″ RADIUS

Fig. 5

THE BENCH

A well designed and strongly built bench is essential and it should be planned and designed to save time and labour. The one illustrated in Fig. 6 has a heavy wooden top bolted to an angle-iron frame; two vices are fitted, a leg vice nearest the hearth for heavy blacksmith's work, and an engineer's vice at the opposite end. It is more convenient to keep tools in boxes on a shelf under the bench than in drawers; the additional weight will help to stabilize the bench. To keep the bench clear of tools when working, a shelf of the type shown in Fig. 6 should be fitted to the wall above the bench. Close against the wall is a strip of wood with $\frac{1}{2}$″ and $\frac{3}{4}$″ holes bored alternately at 2″ intervals to take small tools which would not stand upright in a slot. In front of this is a $\frac{1}{2}$″ slot for the longer tools such as files and screwdrivers, and in front of this again is a broad shelf for tools in current use. The $\frac{1}{2}$″ holes drilled horizontally in the front edge of the broad shelf are for pencils, scribers, centre punches, etc. To keep these holes clear of dirt $\frac{3}{4}$″ holes can be drilled from the underside of the shelf as shown inset in top left corner of Fig. 6. A rack for pliers, shown inset on the right, can be made from two bars of $1″ \times \frac{3}{16}$″ iron about $\frac{3}{4}$″ apart and

4

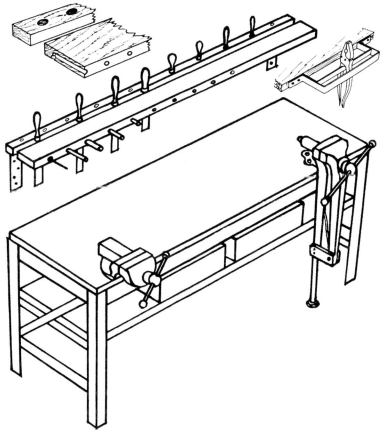

Fig. 6

fixed to the front of the shelf or in any other convenient place. Where space permits, the bench should be backed against the wall on the working side of the hearth and receive natural light from either a window or a skylight. It does not matter if the shelf cuts across the window as the bench will still get the light and, in addition, the tools can be seen easily. If the smith cannot afford to install fluorescent lighting, which is ideal but expensive, ordinary electric lamps for the bench and machines should be fitted on adjustable brackets to give light where it is most needed.

THE VICES

A steel leg vice (Fig. 6) is still the best for smithing. Heavy bending or hammering should always be done in the leg vice, as the strain and shock on the jaws are taken by the leg which is usually let into a steel socket set in the concrete floor.

The parallel jaw or engineer's vice should also be made of steel, and it is an advantage to have a quick release action for the jaws. A cast steel engineer's vice will stand almost anything, but the cheaper malleable variety should only be used for fitting and precision work; it is not designed for heavy hammering or excessive strains on the jaws, and must not be used for these purposes.

TOOL RACKS

One type of rack for taking hardies and anvil swages is shown fitted beneath the hearth in Fig. 2.

Chisels, punches and drifts can be kept within reach of the anvil in another type of rack which is made by drilling a series of $\frac{7}{8}''$ holes in a piece of $2'' \times 2''$ timber secured to the wall or other convenient place with a piece of $2'' \times 1''$ below it, as shown in Fig. 7. In this type of rack both ends of each tool can always be seen; nothing can be lost down the holes, and dirt cannot block them.

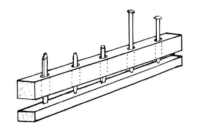

Fig. 7

TONG RACKS

These can be made of round or flat bar and are usually bolted or hung on the water trough where they are near the hearth.

FLOOR MANDREL

The Floor Mandrel (Fig. 8) is a hollow cast-iron cone, often standing breast high, which is used for rounding up small tyres, rings and hoops.

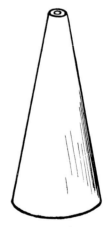

Fig. 8

THE SWAGE BLOCK

The swage block (Fig. 9) is a rectangular block of cast iron with different sizes of half round and V-shaped notches on all four sides and various

6

shaped holes through the face. It is best mounted on a stand which enables any of the edges or the face to be used at a convenient height.

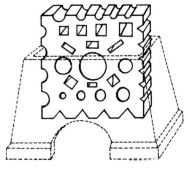

Fig. 9

This completes the essential equipment of a blacksmith's shop. No heights for the bench and anvil have been given because individual craftsmen vary so much in their own heights and opinions. It is a useful guide to know that, when standing normally, you should be able to rest your elbow on the top of the vice. Make up your mind what height suits you best and see that you have it right. It is all too easy to accept the height of a forge, an anvil or a vice as you find it and go on putting up with it without realizing that a small alteration will make life and work much easier for all time.

CHAPTER 2

THE BLACKSMITH'S TOOLS

The blacksmith, unlike many other craftsmen, is able to make most of his own tools, particularly when one is required for a special job.

The principal hand tools are hand and sledge-hammers, a great variety of chisels, punches, drifts and a selection of tongs with differently shaped bits or jaws. For shaping and cutting metal a smith needs tools which fit into the hardy hole in the anvil and others for use under the sledge-hammer. For measuring and marking off, he will want calipers, dividers, a set square and a rule, which should be made of brass; a steel rule soon becomes rusty through being in constant contact with heat and water. Smith's calipers, which have one arm each side and a long handle beyond the joint, are particularly useful.

7

HAMMERS

For everyday forging, blacksmiths use ball-peened hammers varying from 1¾ lb. to 3 lb. in weight. Some prefer short hafts and some very long ones, but it is vital to have a hammer whose balance suits *you*. Do not use one just because it happens to be handy. When you have found a suitable hammer, it is wise to keep a spare which matches it as closely as possible both as to head and haft. Then, if the haft breaks in the middle of an important job, you will not be inconvenienced by suddenly having to use a hammer with a different balance. Although the blacksmith does not usually make his own hammer heads, most smiths have certain special hammers (Fig. 10) for special purposes which they either make themselves or adapt from standard patterns. Car axle half-shafts are suitable material for making special hammer heads.

Fig. 10

TONGS

The beginner must acquire several pairs of ready-made tongs (Fig. 11) for a start. The making of tongs is dealt with in Lesson 37.

Fig. 11

COLD CHISELS

Chisels for cutting cold iron (Fig. 12) are made short and thick and are ground a little more acutely than a right angle. They are needed in various widths with both straight and convex cutting edges.

They are made from steel containing about 0·875 per cent carbon; a lower carbon content than the steel used for taps and dies but higher than that used for picks. Steel of the right kind is commonly sold in octagonal (eight sided) bars; it is wise to buy octagonal steel because it cannot be

8

confused with any other metal even if an end of a bar gets rusty and dirty. It does not pay to make cold chisels out of any odds and ends of steel which come to hand, but it is worth stocking several sizes of the proper steel from $\frac{3}{8}''$ to $\frac{7}{8}''$ across the flats.

The smith may be asked to make cold chisels for special purposes such as chipping castings in preparation for welders or for other tradesmen, particularly bricklayers. These chisels are made in a variety of shapes and tempered to suit particular needs.

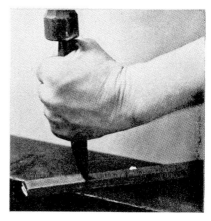

Fig. 12

HOT CHISELS

Chisels for cutting hot iron (Fig. 13) should, by contrast, be made long to keep the hand away from the heat of the job, and slender so that the chisel may be driven into the soft metal like a knife into butter. As the chisel becomes hot it is quenched in water after every three or four blows. A wide variety of shapes and sizes should be kept as a great deal of time can be saved by using hot chisels intelligently.

Some smiths use a sharp cutting edge, but others prefer to leave the edge about $\frac{1}{16}''$ thick.

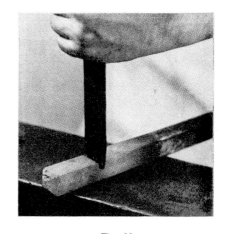

Fig. 13

Hot chisels should be made from steel containing less carbon than cold chisels—0·75 per cent is correct—or preferably from special alloy steels which are now sold for the purpose. Either of these steels can be had in bars $1'' \times \frac{1}{2}''$ with rounded edges. Again it is worth while having this special section so that there is no mistaking it. Although these tools get hot in use, most smiths find it an advantage to temper them.

9

COLD SETS

Cold sets (Fig. 14) are made for use under a sledge-hammer. They are like cold chisels but are even shorter and thicker and are fitted with a handle at one side.

Usually a groove is forged round the middle of the set and either a twisted hazel or an iron rod wrapped round a couple of turns, the ends being left long enough to form a handle. The ends of the hazel rod have an iron ring slipped over them to keep them together; the ends of the iron rod are best welded together in a loop.

Fig. 14

Some cold sets are hafted like hammers which give better control on fine work, but the very severe jars they get in normal service are apt to break the haft or sting the hand.

They can be made from a lower carbon steel than cold chisels, the grade used for swages being quite suitable. The grading of steel is described in Chapter 5.

Fig. 15

HOT SETS

Hot sets (Fig. 15) are the sledge-hammer version of hot chisels and are made from similar material. They are used with more precision than cold sets, so are best hafted like hammers, as the hot iron on which they are used absorbs the shock to a large extent.

10

HARDIES

Hardies are chisels which fit into the square hole in the anvil, the work being driven down onto them (Fig. 16). Some smiths make one fairly stout hardie and use it for both hot and cold work, but it is better practice to have two separate ones suitably shaped and tempered for each purpose.

Fig. 16

PUNCHES FOR HOT WORK

Punches used for hot work (Fig. 17) can be round, square or any other shape to suit requirements. Like hot chisels, they should be long enough to keep the hand away from the heat, or if large, they can be rodded like sets. A slot punch makes a long narrow hole with rounded ends and removes the minimum amount of metal. This hole can be enlarged or opened out by using a drift (see below) without weakening the bar. Round-ended punches called 'bob' punches are used for forming scarfs.

Fig. 17

DRIFTS

Drifts (Fig. 18) are pieces of steel of any required section with a long taper at one end and a short taper at the other; they are driven right through punched holes to enlarge, shape and smooth them.

Fig. 18

11

FULLERS

These tools are like chisels and sets but with rounded noses. They are used for making shoulders before drawing down pins and tenons, for forging special shapes and for drawing the metal in one particular direction.

Small Fullers (Fig. 19) are used in the hand.

Fig. 19

Large Fullers (Fig. 20) are rodded.

Bottom Fullers (Fig. 20) fit in the hardy hole of the anvil.

Fig. 20

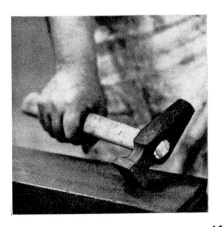

FLATTERS AND SET HAMMERS

These are placed on the work and struck with a sledge. They may have flat or convex faces with sharp or rounded edges, according to the purpose for which they are required (Fig. 21).

Fig. 21

12

SWAGES

Swages are top and bottom tools between which the iron is worked to shape (Fig. 22). The bottom swage fits into the square hole in the anvil and the top swage is handled, and is struck with a sledge- or power-hammer. Swages may be of any form required and are made of the lowest carbon tool steel. A bar of $1\frac{1}{2}''$ square should be kept especially for this and is also suitable for making large sets.

Fig. 22

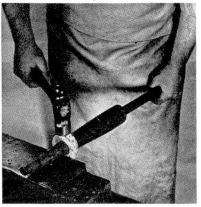

HAND MANDREL

This tool (Fig. 23) is used either on the face or over the edge of the anvil for drawing out and rounding up small rings and collars.

Fig. 23

BOLSTER FOR HARROW TINES

Fig. 24 shows the special bolster used for forming the shoulders on harrow tines. On one side the holes, used for forming the round threaded part, are slightly countersunk to prevent a sudden change of section. The edges of the square holes are raised slightly to produce a concave shoulder on the tine; the prominent edges of these shoulders will then bear hard on the harrow bars when the tine is tightened, thus making a rigid job.

Fig. 24

13

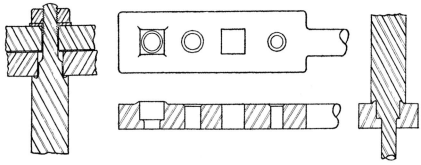

Fig. 25

A cross section of the bolster is shown in the centre of Fig. 25. Below this is a sectional view showing the countersunk edges on the round holes and the upraised shoulder on the square hole.

The right hand drawing shows how the shoulders are formed when the tine is driven into the bolster and the drawing on the left shows the assembly of the tine in the two harrow bars.

CHAPTER 3

THE BLACKSMITH'S FIRE

FUEL

Both coal and coke breeze are used for blacksmithing, and the choice seems to depend mostly on local custom. Although first class work can be done with either, a blacksmith familiar with one is usually embarrassed by the other. Good blacksmithing coal should be bituminous and free from sulphur, and as regular supplies are now hard to obtain the beginner may be well advised to use breeze. This must be good smithy breeze free from dust; the most suitable size is known as 'beans'. Crushed or broken-up boiler coke or furnace coke is not suitable for forging.

14

FIRE TOOLS

Four tools are used to manage the fire: a poker, shovel, rake (Fig. 26) and

Fig. 26

swab (Fig. 27). These vary in more ways than can be imagined. Some blacksmiths never use a rake, and others scorn the swab altogether, but the tools shown are a fair example of a practical set.

Fig. 27

THE FIRE

Coal and coke require slightly different management both in lighting the fire and in keeping it burning properly. To confine the burning part of a coal fire to the required size, soak the coal with water. This will retard combustion, assist coking and impede the passage of the blast. It is not necessary to wet breeze, because its flame does not spread so readily and in any case wetted breeze does not form a draught-proof barrier. As long as enough fresh breeze is fed on to the fire, which must be kept clean, the fire will remain sufficiently concentrated of itself. This difference should be borne in mind when reading the description of managing the fire later in this chapter.

The blacksmith's fire does not burn steadily indefinitely. It gradually

15

builds up to its best, maintains this condition according to the fuel and the work, then dies down until it becomes useless. With good fuel the fire may last all day on rough work, but with poor fuel on fine work it may be dead in an hour. When using coal, make sure before starting a job that an adequate well-soaked supply is available and banked up ready to replenish the fire as required.

Fig. 28 is a sectional view of the fire showing a piece of metal being heated in the heart of the fire and a lump of clinker forming beneath, in front of the tuyere.

Fig. 28

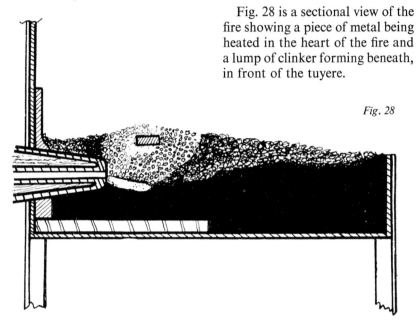

Fig. 29

To light the fire, scoop out a hole in front of the tuyere nose. Remove the clinker (Fig. 29) which is sure to be left over from the last heat and dig out and throw away any excess of dust and fine ash. A coal fire can be lit with nothing but a ball of paper, but a coke fire may need wood shavings or chips. Light the kindling, push the burning part right down by the blast hole, and turn

16

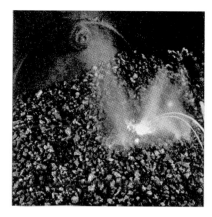

Fig. 30   Fig. 31

on just a mere breath of blast (Fig. 30). As the kindling lights, draw a little dry coke over it (some coke or half-burned coal will always be found in the remains of a coal fire). Gradually increase the blast and as the fire breaks through (Fig. 31) it can be made up directly with fresh breeze. New coal should never be heaped on top of the fire, but always worked in from the outside as in this way the impurities in the coal are burnt away before it comes in contact with the metal. Wet coal should be packed all round and gradually driven into the heart of the fire with the edge of the shovel.

MANAGEMENT OF THE FIRE

There are three aims in managing the fire.

(i) **To keep the fire as small as possible.** The whole purpose of the fire is to heat metal and anything more is both wasteful and a nuisance. Never use more blast than is necessary to keep the fire at the size and heat required for the job.

(ii) **To prevent the fire from burning hollow.** The heat in the fire must be in the middle, immediately below the piece of metal being heated. A hollow fire has no fuel to produce heat where it is wanted. Also the un-burnt blast air will get at the hot metal and oxidize the surface or may even burn it beyond recovery.

(iii) **To defeat clinker.** Clinker is the blacksmith's worst trouble. Cold, clinker is like a crude black glass; hot, it is like black treacle. It is produced by the combination of oxygen in the blast with impurities which are more

17

or less present in all fuels. This is a further reason for not using more blast than necessary.

As the fuel burns, clinker is formed in a molten state and trickles down to the bottom of the fire, just in front of the blast hole. Here the clinker obstructs the blast and bits are blown upwards and stick to the hot metal giving it a molten coating. Metal in this state cannot be welded and when it is struck, the molten clinker spurts out from under the hammer and burns the hands. This not only hurts but interferes with the work.

Unless very good fuel is used, the fire will become dirty almost as soon as it begins to burn freely. At this stage the only thing to do is to persevere for one or two heats in spite of the dirt. The blast is then cut off for a few minutes to allow the liquid clinker to cool and solidify sufficiently to be hooked out in one piece with the tip of the poker, which is flattened and curved for just this purpose (Fig. 32).

A great deal of judgment is required to know exactly how long the clinker must be allowed to cool, when it is ready to catch, and

Fig. 32

just where to find it. Even so, it is a feat of considerable skill to remove it all without disturbing the fire. Nothing but practice is any real help in this. Sometimes the clinker does not form into one lump or else the lump breaks up, but in either case, the pieces can be distinguished from the dully glowing fuel of the cooling fire by their brighter red heat, their smooth surface and, as soon as they begin to cool, by the characteristic 'clink, clink' they make when touched by the fire tools. Hell to a blacksmith is not a place of fire and heat, but of clinker.

The metal which is being heated should be kept near the top of the hot part of the fire with a good bed of live fuel underneath it and a sufficient covering of glowing coke on top. Remember that a coal fire always produces some coke as it burns. This covering not only prevents the heat from being radiated from the metal, but burns up the free oxygen from the air above the fire before it can reach the hot metal and oxidize it.

For this reason metal should never be brought to a red heat on top of the fire—always keep it below the surface where it is protected from the air and where the fire is hotter.

CHAPTER 4

THE BLACKSMITH'S WORK

Blacksmithing consists of working or forging iron and steel at the right heat into the required shape by means of hammer blows delivered either directly onto the metal or transmitted through tools. Parts II, III and IV explain and illustrate in detail each forging operation which may be done singly or in combination. The various processes used are summarized as follows:

TAKING A HEAT

It is very important that the smith should know the signs and the effect of burning iron and that he should be able to recognize instantly the correct degree of temperature which he requires for a particular operation. The instruction 'Take a BRIGHT RED heat' or 'Take a FULL WELDING heat' will be found throughout the lessons and a beginner cannot do better than practice with a bar of iron so that he is able to judge by eye the heat required for a specific purpose.

Always look at the iron in ordinary daylight. Take care by the arrangement of the windows, that the sun's rays cannot fall directly on either the hearth or the anvil as this makes it very difficult to judge the heat of the metal.

WARM HEAT is taken by passing the metal slowly through the fire until it is just too hot to be touched safely by the hand. This is the correct heat for 'setting up' springs without removing the temper.

BLACK HEAT. No red colour is visible in daylight, but the metal will glow faintly red in the dark. This temperature is not used in any smithing operation, but may be used for obtaining an oil or matt black finish on ornamental ironwork.

DULL RED OR BLOOD RED HEAT is used for easy bends on mild steel and for forging carbon steel. It is a little above the temperature required before quenching carbon steel to obtain the maximum hardness.

BRIGHT RED HEAT. Simple forging operations on mild steel are carried out at this temperature: for example, bending over the anvil, light punching and hot chiselling.

BRIGHT YELLOW OR NEAR WELDING HEAT. The principal forging operations on mild steel and wrought iron are carried out at this temperature, including drawing down, upsetting, preparing scarfs and punching on heavy work. This is the correct temperature for forging high-speed steel but carbon steel should not be made so hot.

LIGHT WELDING, SWEATING OR SLIPPERY HEAT. While this is not hot enough for welding many grades of mild steel, it is sometimes used success-fully if difficulty is experienced at higher temperatures. Considerable skill is needed to weld mild steel with a slippery heat.

Wrought iron can be forged at this heat.

FULL WELDING HEAT. If the blast is correct, and the fire has a good heart, a few white bursting sparks will begin to appear among the red sparks from the fire. This is the correct temperature for welding most types of mild steel. *A hollow fire and insufficient blast will produce white sparks, but in this case the surface of the metal is being burnt without attaining the correct welding heat.*

WHITE OR SNOWBALL HEAT is too high for welding mild steel but is the correct heat for welding good quality wrought iron. Wrought iron has a spongy texture at this temperature but will be restored to normal condition by correct forging.

DRAWING DOWN

Drawing down needs a NEAR WELDING heat and is the process of increasing the length of a piece of metal and at the same time reducing its cross section. The simplest example is the formation of a point on a round or square bar by hammering which is described in Lesson 1. On heavy work the drawing down can be done quicker by fullering between top and bottom tools or by using the bick of the anvil as shown in Lesson 9 C.

BENDING

This can sometimes be carried out cold, but it is preferably done at a BRIGHT RED heat. Bends can be made over the anvil or bick, as shown in Lessons 2, 3 and 4, or sometimes on the swage block. The metal on the outside of a bend is subjected to a stretching action while the inside is upset. This is why the square outside corner bend described in Lesson 29 must always be formed by first upsetting the metal to provide the extra material required on the outside.

UPSETTING OR JUMPING UP

This operation, carried out at a NEAR WELDING heat, is for swelling or increasing the cross section of a bar of metal in one particular place, its overall length being reduced at the same time. Considerable practice is required to upset metal exactly in the place where the swelling is needed and the beginner is advised to do the job in easy stages by cooling off the bar with water, leaving just sufficient at the right heat for the first swelling. The bar should be re-heated and upsetting continued to the required amount.

HOT CUTTING

Hot cutting is done with hot chisels and sets; portions of the metal are either cut away completely or, in some cases, a split is made and opened out to receive another piece for welding, as shown in Lessons 5, 20, 31 and 32. A BRIGHT RED heat is best for hot cutting. Cold cutting is described on page 28.

PUNCHING AND DRIFTING

These operations are best carried out with the work at a NEAR WELDING heat. If the hole is deep, the metal tends to contract round the punch which should be withdrawn after every three or four blows and quenched in water. Drifts are used to finish holes that have been punched smaller than the required size and it may be necessary to take two or more heats to complete the job satisfactorily; this is described in Lesson 16. When punching deep holes sprinkle a few grains of fuel into the hole before replacing the punch. The gas formed when the punch is next driven in will blow it out again quickly, saving both time and trouble.

FIRE WELDING

Fire welding is the operation whereby two pieces of metal are joined together while in a plastic state by hammering. Different types of welds are explained in the lessons and considerable practice is required before the simplest fire weld is mastered and even then, some grades of mild steel present difficulties which call for ingenuity in using the right technique. The essential conditions for fire welding are as follows:

(a) Metal properly prepared to suit the type of weld required.

(b) A clinker-free clean fire with a good heart.

(c) Accurate judgment by eye of the correct welding heat which varies from a LIGHT WELDING heat to a WHITE heat with different types of steel and iron.

(d) Speed in withdrawing the metal from the fire and placing the pieces in the correct position on the anvil, followed immediately by rapid and accurate hammer blows delivered on the heated metal at the proper place and in the right order.

Much practice is needed to develop and co-ordinate all these essential factors, the most difficult being the judging of the correct welding heat, which ranges from a bright sparkling white heat for good quality wrought iron down to a bright red just changing to white heat for mild steel.

INSTRUCTIONS FOR FIRE WELDING

The following instructions on fire welding should be read and the procedure thoroughly understood before attempting any of the lessons which include this operation.

c

A certain amount of metal is always lost during fire welding, so it is essential to upset or thicken the ends first. The upset ends are then forged to form scarfs which must 'pair' when laid together. The important factor when shaping a scarf is to make certain that the point of contact between the two pieces is in the middle so that when the metal is hammered, any scale or oxide is squeezed to the outside and not trapped in the centre.

The scarfs should not be so short that they slide apart before they 'take', neither should they be too long or the lips will burn off before the thickened parts reach welding heat.

Although welds can be made without using a flux, it is often an advantage to use either silver sand or one of the preparatory fire welding compounds, such as 'Laffite' Welding Plate.

When using silver sand, the pieces to be welded are placed in the fire side by side with the faces of the scarfs *downwards* and brought to a NEAR WELDING heat. Each piece in turn is then removed from the fire for a moment and the face of the scarf sprinkled with a little silver sand which immediately melts and flows over the iron, fluxing any scale or oxide that may have begun to form. Both pieces are then returned to the fire still face down and are jockeyed about a little to get a heat on each evenly.

The following actions have to be done much more quickly than they can be described. Immediately welding heat is reached the first piece is removed from the fire still with the scarf face downward. It is tapped over the edge of the anvil to shake off the melted sand and dirt clinging to it and immediately turned over and laid face upward on the anvil.

The second piece is also taken from the fire face downward, similarly tapped over the edge of the anvil to shake off the dirt, and, without turning it over, placed in position on top of the first piece. The first blow is then struck in the centre of the weld.

Some experienced smiths can tell from the sound of the first few hammer blows if the weld has taken or not. A dense or hard ringing note indicates that the weld has not taken. It is quite permissible to take a second welding heat to close the ends of the scarfs as these cool off much more quickly than the thicker section of the metal, particularly the bottom one which is in contact with the cold anvil face.

If Laffite is used, the procedure is a little different—when the prepared parts are heated to a DULL RED heat they are removed from the fire and a piece of Laffite plate, a little bigger than the area of the weld, is placed between the scarfs and squeezed with light hammer blows until it melts and spreads over the scarf faces which will stick together. The adhering pieces are then carefully returned to the fire and brought to a LIGHT WELDING heat when they are lifted out and given a few gentle blows with

22

the hammer to unite them. They are then returned to the fire for another LIGHT WELDING heat and the job finished off with ease and certainty.

HEAT TREATMENT

Heat treatment is applied to steel to make it harder, tougher or softer as required. These qualities depend on the composition of the steel combined with the heat treatment it receives (see Chapter 5 on Blacksmith's Materials). Although an open fire is not an ideal method of carrying out all these processes, there are five types of heat treatment that the blacksmith frequently undertakes on small articles, and the following brief descriptions are only intended to explain the meaning of the terms used. More detailed information should be obtained by studying the relevant chapters in the books listed at the end of this publication (page 104).

Hardening is carried out by heating medium and high carbon steels slowly and uniformly to the correct temperature between BLACK and DULL RED heat and then quenching them suddenly in some suitable cooling medium, such as water, oil or brine, according to the composition of the steel and the degree of hardness required.

Tempering. Carbon steel that has been hardened by quenching as described, is very brittle and in this state is useless for cutting tools, particularly those which are subjected to blows. Some of this hardness must be sacrificed to obtain the requisite toughness and this is done by re-heating the metal to a lower temperature than that required for hardening and cooling rather more gently in the cooling medium. The degree of temper required is obtained by controlling the temperature to which the metal is re-heated and varies from a high or hard temper for small edge tools to a low or soft temper for certain kinds of springs.

Annealing is a softening process carried out by heating steel to the correct temperature and then allowing it to cool slowly in a dying fire or by burying the metal under hot ashes or in dry lime.

Normalizing differs from annealing in that although the metal is raised to the same temperature, it is allowed to cool off naturally in the air. It should not be laid on a cold floor or other cold surface or exposed to draughts when cooling. It is an advantage to normalize any steel which has been forged or welded, before the article is put into service.

Case Hardening is a process by which a hard skin is obtained on steel which does not contain enough carbon to make it harden by heating and quenching. It is carried out by packing the article to be case-hardened in a suitable metal container with a special case hardening compound, such as 'Kasenit', and then heating the whole container to a RED heat (900° Cent.) and letting it soak at this temperature for a given period before allowing it to cool slowly. The carbon in the

23

compound penetrates the skin of the metal and unites with the steel to produce a dead hard surface when the article is subsequently hardened by re-heating and rapid quenching.

CHAPTER 5

THE BLACKSMITH'S MATERIALS

WROUGHT IRON

Wrought iron has long been regarded as the traditional material worked by the blacksmith, and its replacement by mild steel for most forging is still a matter of regret amongst older craftsmen whose early experience did not include the forging and welding of mild steel, which requires modified techniques.

Wrought iron, which is produced by puddling pig iron in a special hearth, is more expensive than mild steel. Commercial wrought iron contains approximately 0·04 per cent carbon and 0·2 per cent slag which, during the process of manufacture, is hammered or squeezed throughout the mass of the metal, producing the well-known fibrous structure which makes wrought iron so easily recognizable when broken across the grain. Two of the vital qualities possessed by wrought iron are its ability to be drawn out—'ductility', and its ability to be hammered into shapes—'malleability'.

Iron which is malleable is not necessarily ductile and iron which possesses either of these qualities when cold does not necessarily possess them when hot, and vice versa.

Iron which is apt to break when cold is called 'cold short' and iron which is apt to break when hot is called 'red short'. These most undesirable qualities are caused by impurities in the metal, excess of phosphorus and sulphur making it cold short and excess of silicon making it red short.

Due to its low carbon content, wrought iron is highly malleable and ductile and is easily forged and welded by the blacksmith. It was once used

24

extensively for all types of constructional work, but it is now confined to a few special uses in industry where ductility and resistance to corrosion are required rather than high tensile strength.

It is these special characteristics, however, which make wrought iron eminently suitable for decorative iron work, for which it is still preferred by many blacksmiths. The texture of wrought iron improves with careful forging and it can be worked and welded into the most intricate, delicate and graceful shapes with greater ease than mild steel.

Wrought iron can be worked at a wider range of heat than is possible with mild steel so that despite its high cost, a small stock of wrought iron is particularly valuable for tricky jobs. For example, a small collar for welding onto a steel shank, is better made of wrought iron as it is able to withstand the extra heat which the collar naturally gets before the whole job is at the correct temperature for welding.

Steel is a general term applied to alloys of pure iron and carbon. The *quality* of steel is determined by the selection of iron and alloying ingredients used in its manufacture and not by its carbon content, or by the appearance of the fracture. The *temper* of steel refers to the carbon content and has nothing to do with quality. The term should not be confused with 'tempering', which is used in connection with the Heat Treatment described in Chapter 4. Detailed information on the tempering of carbon steels will be found in Balfour's 'Hints on Steel' listed at the end of the book (page 104).

MILD STEEL

Mild steel which contains from $0 \cdot 2$ per cent to $0 \cdot 3$ per cent carbon, can be readily forged and welded within a narrower range of temperatures than wrought iron. It is less ductile and malleable than wrought iron but possesses greater tensile strength, which is an essential characteristic for the majority of forgings. It cannot be hardened or tempered and when fractured it shows a granular or non-fibrous structure.

MEDIUM CARBON STEEL

Medium carbon steel contains from $0 \cdot 5$ per cent to $0 \cdot 6$ per cent carbon and is harder and stronger than mild steel, being readily forged but not so easily welded. While it cannot be tempered to hold a cutting edge, it can be hardened to a certain degree.

HIGH CARBON STEEL

High carbon steel contains from $0 \cdot 75$ per cent to $1 \cdot 5$ per cent carbon and can be hardened to a high degree and tempered to retain a cutting edge.

When working high carbon steels in the forge, great care must be taken because they have a comparatively narrow range of forging and heat treatment temperatures, being easily oxidized or burnt beyond recovery. High carbon steel is usually graded into six tempers according to its carbon content. Various manufacturers have their own system of classification; the following is probably most common and is used by Arthur Balfour & Co. Ltd.

Temper No. 5. (0·875 per cent carbon) is the one most suitable for blacksmiths' and fitters' cutting tools, such as cold chisels, sets, etc.

Temper No. 6. (0·75 per cent carbon) is used for making hammer heads, hot sets, punches and drifts.

ALLOY STEELS

Alloy steels include a great variety of steels containing, in addition to carbon, other constituents which give them special characteristics.

It is not within the scope of this book to describe the chemical contents or the physical and mechanical properties of the many types of steel and the student is recommended to read the special books on this subject which are listed on page 104.

Note: The word 'metal' is used throughout this book to denote either wrought iron or steel. If either is intended as distinct from the other, it is mentioned by name.

PART II

PART II

Part I described the blacksmith's shop with its equipment and tools, fuel and fire and the processes he uses in his work. The student is now ready to begin practical work; the first twelve lessons provide him with elementary exercises in smithing, which include simple forging and welding on light materials.

In every lesson the material to be used must be cut to the required length, and although metal of heavy section is not dealt with until later in the book, the instructions for cutting both light and heavy sections are given here.

Cutting off cold metal of Light Section

Light section bars may be cut either with a cold chisel or over a hardie. It is not necessary to cut right through the bar. Nicks should be made evenly round the bar as shown in Fig. 33, so that the end may be easily dressed. The bar can then be snapped either by hammering it over the far side of the anvil as shown in Fig. 34, if the end is fairly short, or otherwise by striking the bar itself over the edge of the anvil. When cutting short lengths take care that the end does not fly up and hit you in the eye.

Fig. 33

Fig. 34

28

Cutting off cold metal of Heavy Section

When cutting heavy sections use a cold set and sledge hammer; a striker will be needed and again, it is unnecessary to cut right through the bar; nicking all round is sufficient. This is shown in Fig. 35. If the bar is to be upset it is an advantage to dress the ends as shown in Fig. 36. This will prevent excess swelling at the tip and, by centralizing the force of the blow, reduce the tendency of the bar to buckle.

Fig. 35   *Fig. 36*

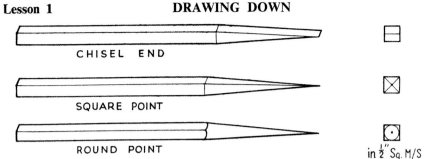

CHISEL END

SQUARE POINT

ROUND POINT

in $\frac{1''}{2}$ Sq. M/S

HOLDING THE HAMMER

It needs practice to hit the metal in the right place.

Holding the hammer properly helps, so grip it like this near the end of the haft and swing the blow freely from the elbow *not* from the shoulder.

Don't 'choke' the hammer by gripping it right under the head.

CHISEL END

Take a NEAR WELDING heat on the piece.

Hold it on the anvil face at a slight angle. Hammer it at a steeper angle towards the tongs. This will thin and spread the end.

Don't try to push the metal with the hammer, hit it fair and square.

After one or two blows turn the piece on its side, hold it flat on the anvil and correct the spreading.

Keep on forging first on the flat and then on the side, beginning at the tip and working backwards until it is finished.

A

B

C

Lesson 1—*cont.*

SQUARE POINT

The vital thing in forging a square point is a quick and accurate right angle turn of the wrist between blows.

Look at the hand holding the tongs, first this way—

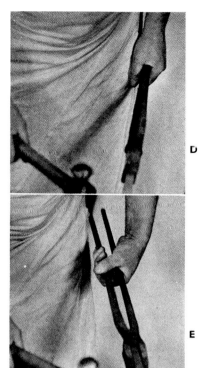

Then like this—

Notice the quarter turn of the wrist.

Take a LIGHT WELDING heat each time the metal is re-heated so that any tendency to split is counteracted by the subsequent blows.

Draw to an abrupt point first, then work it backwards until the point is 3″ long.

Note: When drawing heavy sections, work over the top of the bick, as this gives a fullering action, and draws the metal faster. (See Lesson 9 C.) Then finish the point on the flat of the anvil like this—

ROUND POINT

To make a round point from either round or square bars, it is necessary to make a square point first. Then hammer in each corner to make the point eight-sided as shown here—

Next, round up the point.

31

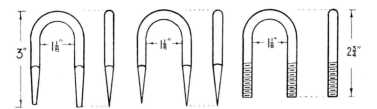

Staple in 5/16″ Rd. M/S
'U' Bolt in ½″ Rd. M/S

CHAIN STAPLE

Cut off 7″ of $\frac{5}{16}$″ Rd. M/S.

Take a NEAR WELDING heat and draw down the points as shown in Lesson 1.

At a BRIGHT RED heat, start forming the bend around the bick of the anvil, keeping the points in line.

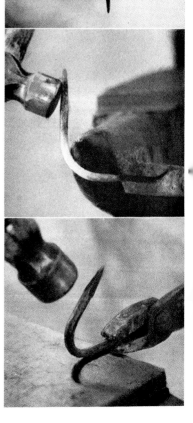

Continue bending the piece like this to an even semi-circle, still keeping the points in line.

The beginner can test the radius on a piece of $1\frac{1}{8}$″ diameter round bar to check his eye.

Finish like this—

Leave one point a little longer than the other as this helps to position the staple correctly when driving it into the wood.

U-BOLT

Cut off 7″ of ½″ Rd. M/S.

To make the U-bolt, first chamfer the ends like this—

Then bend to shape as with the staple.

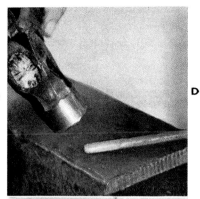

D

Grip one end in the vice and twist the middle of the U so that the ends are nearly at right angles as shown here—

This allows room to rotate the die stock.

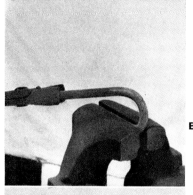

E

Allow to cool before threading the ends.

Then twist it back into a U shape and true up with light hammer blows when the bolt is lying flat on the anvil face.

F

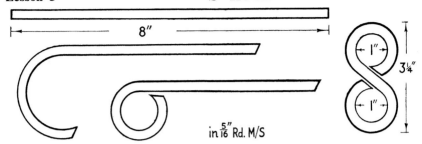

in $\frac{5}{16}$" Rd. M/S

Take a BRIGHT RED heat and, holding the end of the bar flat on the anvil face, dress to a short bevel with the hammer like this—

The ends will then close snugly to the middle of the hook when the eyes are closed.

Start to form the first eye by striking the end over the bick like this and continue as in Lesson 2 B.

Repeat on the other end, but with the eye in the opposite direction.

This is the finished hook, with both eyes equal.

Test them over a piece of 1" diameter round bar and leave the hooks open as shown until the S hook is needed for use.

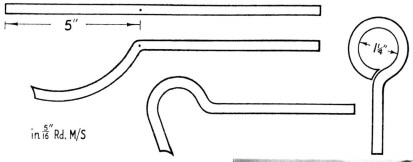

in $\frac{5}{16}''$ Rd. M/S

Mark off 5″ from one end of the bar as shown in the drawing.

Take a BRIGHT RED heat and place the mark on the rounded edge of the anvil. The first blows with the hammer should be straight downwards and then at this angle—

With each blow the free end will jerk upwards and start to form the bend for the eye.

Take another heat on the partly formed second bend. Cool out the first bend with water and continue to form eye like this—

Finish the eye over the bick.

Close up by tapping lightly around the outside of the eye and test by trying it over a piece of 1¼″ diameter round bar.

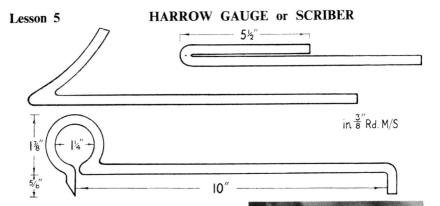

$5\frac{1}{2}''$

in $\frac{3}{8}''$ Rd. M/S

$1\frac{7}{8}''$ $1\frac{1}{4}''$

$\frac{5}{16}''$

$10''$

Before forming the eye, the acute bend at the root of the loop must be strengthened by adding extra metal in the form of a small wedge, made from $\frac{3}{8}''$ round bar, welded into the rod.

At a BRIGHT RED heat, the wedge is first drawn to a chisel point so—

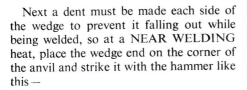

Next a dent must be made each side of the wedge to prevent it falling out while being welded, so at a NEAR WELDING heat, place the wedge end on the corner of the anvil and strike it with the hammer like this —

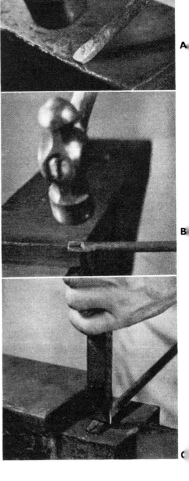

Lay the wedge end on the anvil table and cut off about $\frac{1}{2}''$ with a hot chisel.

Mark the $\frac{3}{8}''$ rod with a centre punch $5\frac{1}{2}''$ from the end.

Take a NEAR WELDING heat and bend at this mark to a hairpin shape.

Force in the wedge and close the hairpin to grip it tightly.

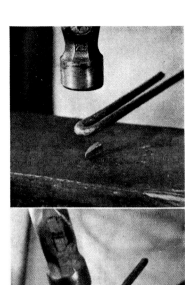

D

Clean the fire and take a FULL WELDING heat. Hold the bar with the short leg of the hairpin standing up thus—

Weld in the wedge with moderate blows delivered at the angle shown.

Turn the hairpin flat and hammer in the sides.

E

Use a small hot chisel with a curved cutting edge to trim away the surplus metal leaving a neatly radiused corner.

This is much stronger than a rough and ragged edge as, with a smooth flowing curve, there is nothing to start a crack.

F

Take another heat on the short end and start to bend in over the bick like this— then turn it over as in Lesson 4 C to close the eye to the shape as shown in the next illustration, H.

G

Here is the eye completed—

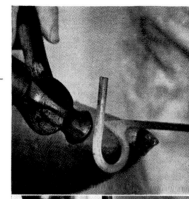

Flatten the end as shown in the drawing.

To complete the scriber, heat the other end, bend it to the dimensions given, like this—

And then cut off to match the point as shown in the drawing.

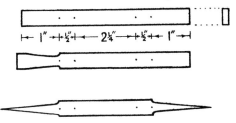

in $\frac{1}{2}'' \times \frac{3}{16}''$ Flat M/S

Cut off 5¼″ from a piece of ½″ × ³⁄₁₆″ flat, and mark it at 1″ and 1½″ from each end.

Take a NEAR WELDING heat and with the punch mark nearest the end over the near edge of the anvil, forge a shoulder by striking with the heel of the hammer like this—

Draw the end to a point and then repeat on the other end.

A

To prevent the sharp edge of the vice jaw from galling or cracking the inside of the bends, use vice jaw clamps with rounded top edges.

Take a BRIGHT RED heat and grip in the vice with the second mark on the edge of the clamp. To make the corner as square as possible, first pull the end down with the tongs, leaving an arch so—

B

Next hammer the arch back towards the corner. In the picture the hammer is not only coming down but also moving bodily to the right. This is described as a drawing blow.

Heat the other end and repeat.

C

39

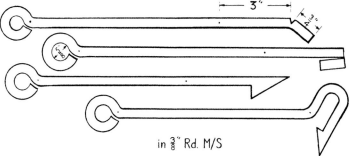

in $\frac{3}{8}''$ Rd. M/S

Take a piece of $\frac{3}{8}''$ round mild steel 10″ long and bend one end into a tight eye with an inside diameter of $\frac{5}{8}''$.

Mark off $3\frac{3}{4}''$ from the other end and, at a BRIGHT RED heat make a nick with a chisel $\frac{1}{4}''$ from the end and double the end right back.

A

Take a FULL WELDING heat on the doubled end and weld with medium blows, drawing the tip to a chisel end. Leave the top shoulder of the barb sharp and square with both sides flat, like this—

B

This is the finished end.

Re-heat to BRIGHT RED and with the punch mark on the edge of the anvil, bend to a right angle with the head of the barb outside. To complete the hook, turn to a semi-circle as shown in the drawing.

Make sure that the hook and the eye are in line.

C

40

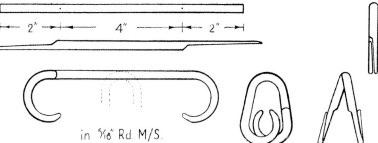

in ⁵⁄₁₆″ Rd. M/S.

Cut off 8″ of $\frac{5}{16}$″ Rd. and mark off at 2″ from each end.

At a NEAR WELDING heat, draw the ends of the rod to blunt points.

Next using a bottom swage, forge each end to a half round section, as far as the punch mark.

A

At a BRIGHT RED heat, turn each end to exactly the same radius, so that they will pair up evenly when set together.

B

Re-heat if necessary, and bend the centre over the bick, leaving the ends matched up but $\frac{1}{4}$″ apart.

When the split ends are closed together they should be very little thicker than the rest of the link.

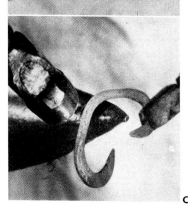

C

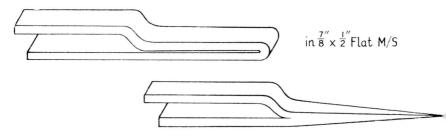

in $\frac{7''}{8} \times \frac{1''}{2}$ Flat M/S

One end of the bar is first offset so that it may be held more conveniently in the tongs.

Take a BRIGHT RED heat, and double the bar back to a tight hairpin.

A

Clean the fire.

Take a FULL WELDING heat, lay the bar flat on the anvil face and weld with heavy blows, working from the bend backward to drive out clinker. Work quickly over the end and make sure the back is welded soundly. A second heat may be required.

B

Test the weld by drawing down to a long square point.

Metal of this size should first be forged over the anvil bick as the curved surface of the bick will tend to draw it length-wise. The drawing down will, consequently, be completed quickly as there will be little sideways spread.

In drawing down heavy sections, large fullers can be used instead of the anvil bick.

C

Finish the point by forging on the anvil face like this—

A defective weld will split while being drawn down.

D

When cold, make a further test by dropping the point into a suitable hole in the swage block. Drive a wedge down between the unwelded parts and hammer them apart. A defective weld will open up as shown with the piece lying in the foreground.

E

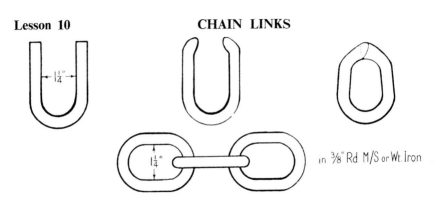

in ⅜″ Rd M/S or Wt. Iron

From a piece of ¾″ round cut off 6″, and bend it to a U shape as in Lesson 2.

It may help a beginner who is inexperienced in fire welding to upset, or thicken, the end slightly before bending the U. (See Lessons 13 and 24.)

At a NEAR WELDING heat, draw out the scarfs cornerwise, like this—

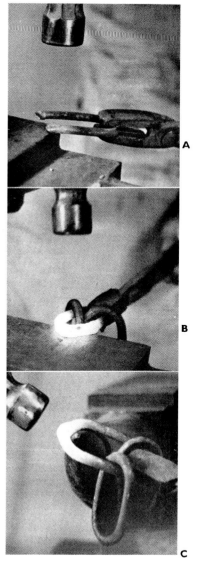

Bend each end towards the other until the scarfs overlap, then set together ready to weld.

When joining or building up a chain, the completed links must be threaded over the unwelded link before setting the scarfs together.

Clean the fire.

Take a FULL WELDING heat and, with light blows, weld on top of the anvil, like this—

Work up on the bick, leaving the welds slightly larger than the original diameter of metal. This is shown in the weld on the top of the finished link hanging next to the tongs.

Lesson 10—*cont.*

Here are three finished chain links.

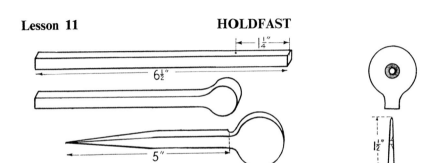

in ⅜″ Sq. M/S.

Take a ⅜″ square bar about 18″ long and mark off 6½″, but do not cut it. Take a NEAR WELDING heat on the end nearest the mark.

To produce a clean shoulder to the swelling quench by pouring water over the bar, thus confining the heat to the last 1¼″. Upset the end by driving the bar down on to the anvil until the end is as broad as it is long, i.e., about ⅞″ in each way.

Hold the bar level with the anvil top and forge in the corners with hammer blows, holding the hammer at an angle of 45°. Flatten the sides as you go.

Take a fresh heat if necessary and continue shaping up the knob with the shoulder over the rounded edge of the anvil. To keep a well defined shoulder to the knob, hold the left hand well below the level of the anvil face.

Give the bar a quarter of a turn and bring the hand level with the anvil top. With the knob only on the anvil face hammer it into an offset disc, the top side of which must be flush with the bar and the under side stepped to the part which will form the shank.

D

Next turn the disc on edge and, keeping it on the same part of the anvil, finish to a good shape by raising and lowering the bar as you strike like this—

When finished, the disc should be about $1\frac{1}{2}''$ in diameter $\times$ $\frac{3}{16}''$ thick.

Do not bend the disc over yet or you will find it difficult to hold when drawing the point.

E

Take a **BRIGHT RED** heat at the mark on the bar, and cut off on the anvil table with a hot chisel. Take a second heat and, with the disc end held in the tongs, draw the other end down to a chisel point, slightly tapered on the sides like this—

F

With the step uppermost, bend the disc to a right angle over the rounded edge of the anvil, flattening the outside of the disc to the shoulder as shown in the drawing.

G

PIPE HOOK

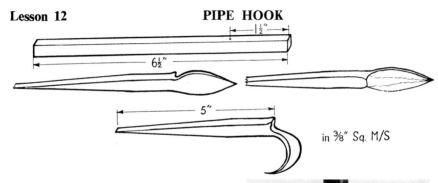

in ⅜" Sq. M/S

To form the bold shoulder which is required so that the clamp may be driven into the wall, take a NEAR WELDING heat and make a groove with a hand fuller at about $1\frac{1}{2}$" from the end.

Using the same heat, draw the end to a fine square point and then flatten it back to the groove to form a shoulder.

The flattened end should look something like a spearhead 3" long with a rib down the middle.

Take a DULL RED heat and cut off to the required length. Holding the flattened end in the tongs take a NEAR WELDING heat and draw to a long chisel point. Then with the point in the tongs, finish the hook by bending the flattened part over the bick like this—

Test over a 1" bore pipe.

PART III

PART III

Having completed the first twelve lessons the student should have sufficient skill to undertake the forging and welding of heavier sectioned metal. The next exercises are designed to develop accuracy in forging to dimensions. He will have learnt for himself that all smithing operations need a great deal of practice and that he cannot expect to complete any of the exercises perfectly the first time. It needs considerable practice to distinguish the various heats, to hit the metal accurately and to deliver the blows at exactly the angle required.

It cannot be stressed too often that the processes described in this book are not the only ones which are used by smiths. Most men evolve their own techniques, others adopt the methods which have been used in their own locality for generations. The techniques described here are considered by the Council for Small Industries in Rural Areas the best for the student to learn; and are those used by the Council's instructors.

Welded rings and chain links are included in this section; the following general instructions on rings and the method of calculating the amount of material required should be carefully studied.

RINGS

Rings which the blacksmith has to make fall roughly into three categories:

(1) **Rings bent on the edge,** ranging from washers to waggon sweeps (the rings on which the fore-carriage turns).

(2) **Rings bent on the flat,** ranging from ferrules to cart-wheel tyres.

(3) **Rings of round and square section** of various sizes.

Fig. 37

Metal up to $\frac{3}{8}''$ round or square need not be upset before scarfing the ends as the welds can be made very quickly without wastage. All flat metal and round and square section above $\frac{3}{8}''$ must be upset before scarfing.

Square and round section metal must be scarfed so that the welding begins with the ring flat on the face of the anvil. In the case of a small ring, welding is continued with the ring over the bick, and with a large ring, from the inside with the ring standing upright on the anvil face.

After welding, small rings are rounded up on a hand mandrel (Fig. 23, page 13), and larger ones on a blacksmith's floor mandrel (Fig. 8, page 6).

To Calculate the Amount of Metal Required

When measuring off a bar which is to be bent into a ring, some allowances have to be made for the metal lost—both in the bending and the welding. Most smiths have their own methods of estimating these allowances, but a beginner needs some simple practical system, such as the following, on which to base his calculations.

(*a*) To determine the allowance for *bending*, add the thickness of the metal to the *inside* diameter of the finished ring, and multiply this figure by $3\frac{1}{7}$.

(*b*) To determine the allowance for *welding*, take the final figure arrived at above, and add twice the thickness of the metal.

For example

To find the length of the metal required for a ring (shown in Lesson 14) with an *inside* diameter of 6″, made in metal $\frac{1}{2}$″ thick:

A.	Inside diameter of ring		6″
	Thickness of metal		$\frac{1}{2}$″
	Total	=	$6\frac{1}{2}$″
	Multiply $6\frac{1}{2}$″ × $3\frac{1}{7}$ (π)	=	$20\frac{3}{8}$″ (approx.)
B.	Add twice the thickness		1″
	Amount required	=	$21\frac{3}{8}$″

51

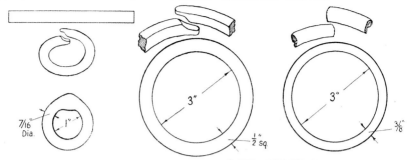

THE SMALL RING

The ring is to be welded on to a shank in Lesson 33, so extra metal must be left in the first weld to form the scarf for the later welding operation.

Using the formula on page 51, calculate and cut off the material required.

Take a NEAR WELDING heat on one end and, holding the bar vertically with the hot end on the anvil face, upset the end by striking the top as shown here—

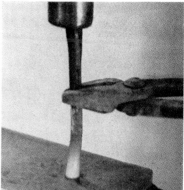

The middle of the bar will buckle slightly.

After every two or three upsetting blows on the top, straighten out the buckle in this way—

Heat the other end and upset in the same way.

Take a BRIGHT RED heat and form the ring over the bick, leaving the ends for scarfing like this—

At a NEAR WELDING heat, using the corner of the anvil to give the required offset, form a scarf at each end on opposite sides so that they pair up when laid over each other.

D

Set the scarfs down tight like this— Then dress up the joint over the bick with light hammer blows.

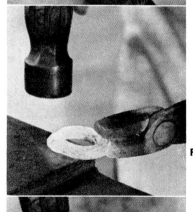

E

Take a FULL WELDING heat and weld first on the face of the anvil like this—

As soon as the weld feels solid, transfer the ring to the bick of the anvil.

F

Finish the weld over the point of the bick like this—

Note the extra metal left in the weld.

This and the preceding operation must be done in the same heat, so work quickly.

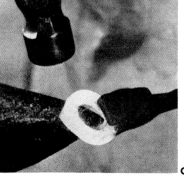

G

THE 3″ DIAMETER RINGS

Cut off the required amount of metal from a ½″ *square* bar.

The ends must be upset before bending and scarfing as described for the small ring made in the first exercise in this lesson.

Set the scarfs together on the anvil face and align the ends on the bick as shown here.

Weld as before.

By this time the student should be practised enough to weld a ring from ⅜″ round without upsetting the ends.

Calculate the amount of metal and cut off the required piece.

Bend the ring into shape and form the scarfs on the plain ends like this—

Make sure they are on opposite sides.

Set the scarfs together and align the ends thus—

Then weld as in the previous exercises.

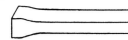

in 1" x ½" Flat M/S

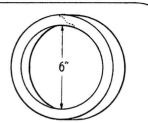

6"

Calculate the length of material required using the formula given on page 51.

A ring made from this size material requires more upset on both ends. This can be done by either 'tamping' or end hammering according to the length of the bar.

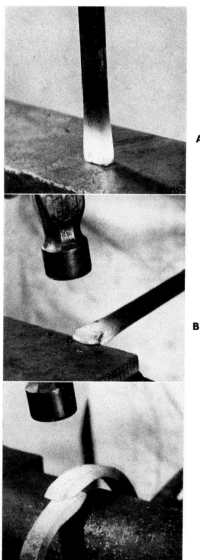

A

Using the rounded edge of the anvil, scarf the ends on opposite sides so that they pair up when laid together.

B

Set the scarfs together over the bick and square up the ends on the face of the anvil before welding.

Take a FULL WELDING heat and start welding on the bick and complete on the flat of the anvil.

C

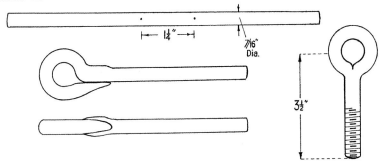

Cut off a piece of $\frac{7}{16}''$ bar $6\frac{1}{2}''$ long by nicking both sides with a cold chisel to give an even-sided end. A sheared cut is always one-sided, producing an uneven end which would cause the bar to skew and bend when being struck on the top for upsetting. See illustration D on the opposite page.

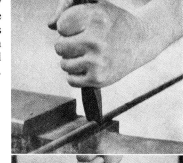

A

Make the first mark on the bar $3''$ from one end, and the second mark $1\frac{1}{4}''$ from the first.

Take a NEAR WELDING heat between the punch marks.

To restrict the heat between the two marks, cool out from the end to the first mark by dipping in water, like this—

B

Cool beyond the second mark by pouring water from a tin as shown—

Both cooling operations must be done quickly to keep the maximum heat between the marks.

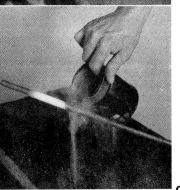

C

Lesson 15—*cont.*

To upset the hot portion, hold the bar vertically on anvil and strike the top like this—

After every two or three blows straighten the resultant buckling on the anvil face and then continue upsetting until the diameter is increased to $\frac{9}{16}''$.

Take a NEAR WELDING heat on the short end and draw to a blunt point to form a scarf.

Bend this end from the upset portion over a $\frac{3}{4}''$ diameter drift like this—

Take a FULL WELDING heat and weld the scarf into the shank with the bend of the eye over the rounded edge of the anvil like this—

Round up the weld with light hammer blows, leaving a radius where the eye joins the shank.

Work up the eye on the bick, leaving a slight V in the junction of the weld, like this—

Don't use a swage to round up the weld as this may weaken the eye by cutting into the radius where the ring joins the shank.

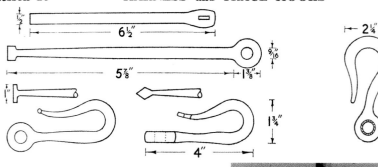

TO PUNCH THE EYE

Take a NEAR WELDING heat on one end of the bar and upset in the swage until the end is bulb shaped:

$1\frac{3}{8}$" long × 1" wide on $\frac{1}{2}$" bar for the harness hook;

$1\frac{3}{8}$" long × $1\frac{1}{4}$" wide on $\frac{5}{8}$" bar for the trace hook.

Flatten the bulb on the anvil face to form a flat knob.

$\frac{9}{16}$" thick on $\frac{1}{2}$" bar.

$\frac{11}{16}$" thick on $\frac{5}{8}$" bar.

Next place a slot punch on the knob, in line with the shank but rather nearer the shoulder than the end. Drive it rapidly through the hot metal until the punch stops against the hard, thin layer on the under side which has been compressed and chilled against the anvil face.

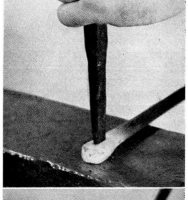

Now, without losing a moment, pull out the punch, and turn the metal over. A black spot will be seen at the blind end of the punch hole. Flick the hot end of the punch immediately into the water trough, and drive it into this black spot until the end breaks through to the other side.

A thin sliver of metal, the size of the hole, will be punched out clean and driven right through.

It can be seen just in front of the glowing knob.

D

Next continue upsetting the end in a larger swage.

This will increase the diameter of the eye and convert the slot into a square hole.

E

To round up the square hole, place the eye over the round hole in the anvil face and drive a drift through.

The end is now almost perfect in shape and a little working up over the bick will produce an eye with nicely chamfered edges all round.

To prevent the edges from cutting the chain link which passes through the hole of the trace hook both sides of the eye must now be countersunk slightly over the bick of the anvil, like this—

The eyes in the harness hooks must *not* be countersunk or the hooks will ride over the corners of the shaft staple.

F

G

Harness Hooks

The **T** and diamond ends on harness hooks are both started with the same operation.

Take a NEAR WELDING heat and make a groove each side $\frac{1}{4}''$ from the end. Use a top hand fuller and a bottom fuller made from $\frac{1}{4}''$ round bar cranked as shown to lie flat on the anvil. The resulting knob should be a little shorter than it is wide. Make sure it is in line with the eye like this one—

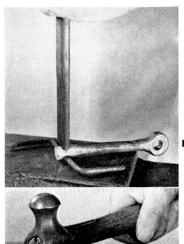

With the groove on the rounded edge of the anvil, forge first to a square and then to a round, easy taper $1\frac{1}{4}''$ long. A hammer with a nicely rounded edge to the flat face should be used to avoid damaging the end or breaking it off.

The next operation varies according to the type of end required.

To make the T end

Grip the tapered part in the vice with the knob on the jaws and form a **T** like this—

Make sure that the sharp edge of the vice jaw does not cut into the shoulders of the **T** and weaken the corners.

Take a fresh heat and work the **T** to a neat round section on the rounded edge of the anvil.

Great care must be taken with both this and the previous forging in the vice; otherwise the **T** will break off or be weakened by nicking under the head.

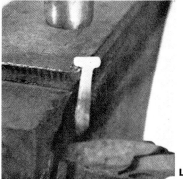

To make the Diamond End

Start the diamond end by fullering and then forging the taper in the same way as for the **T**. *Do not* upset in the vice but forge the end on the anvil to a diamond shape like this—

Keep the flat of the diamond at right angles to the eye and leave a nice curve to the tapered part.

M

Trace Hook

The trace hook with the countersunk eye has a long tapered end which is drawn down and given a slight curve outward as shown here—

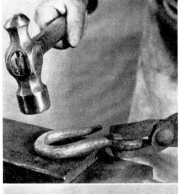

N

Then flatten the centre of the bend slightly to increase the strength.

Give the trace hook a little more flattening round the curve than the others.

All hooks are bent round the bick of the anvil.

O

Compare the measurements on the drawing with the hooks, which should look like this—

P

61

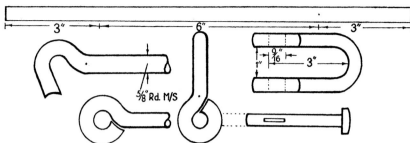

Cut off 12″ from a ⅝″ round bar and mark off as shown in the drawing.

Take a NEAR WELDING heat and lay the bar with the punch mark over the rounded edge of anvil. As this will be a small eye in thick metal, use the ball-peen of the hammer to make the first bend at the shoulder of the eye.

The free end will jerk upwards as described in Lesson 4.

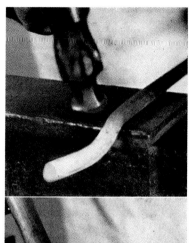

A

Take another NEAR WELDING heat and cool out the bar at the first bend.

Continue turning the eye around the bick—first over the top, then from the underside as in Lesson 4 C.

B

Next trim the end of the eye with a curved hot chisel to form a radius which will fit snugly against the curve of the first bend.

The finished shackle can be seen in the illustration E on the opposite page.

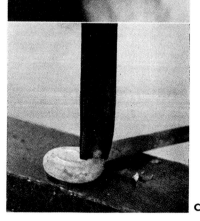

C

With the eye in the bottom swage, close the end of eye down to the first bend by hammering it like this—

The hole should be $\frac{9}{16}''$ in diameter when finished.

Next turn the other eye in the opposite direction, but keep them both in alignment on the bar.

D

Bend the middle of bar round the bick to an even semi-circle to form a **D**, keeping the eyes in alignment as shown in this finished shackle—

The advantage of trimming the ends of the eyes is very plain.

The mushroom-headed pin for this shackle is made in Lesson 19.

E

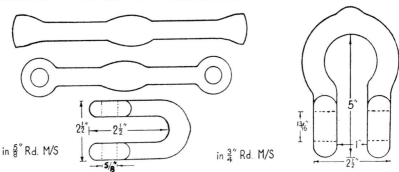

in $\frac{5}{8}''$ Rd. M/S   in $\frac{3}{4}''$ Rd. M/S

Cut off 9″ of $\frac{5}{8}''$ round for the **D** shackle and 14″ of $\frac{3}{4}''$ round for the bow shackle.

First upset each end as in Lesson 16 to a little over twice the thickness of the bar.

Next take a NEAR WELDING heat in the middle of the bar and, with the bottom end in the swage, upset to about $1\frac{1}{2}$ times the original diameter.

Flatten the ends into bosses:
     $1\frac{1}{4}''$ long × $1\frac{1}{8}''$ wide × $\frac{11}{16}''$ thick on the $\frac{5}{8}''$ round.
     $1\frac{1}{2}''$ long × $1\frac{1}{4}''$ wide × $\frac{13}{16}''$ thick on the $\frac{3}{4}''$ round.

Next slot punch and drift the holes to:
     $\frac{5}{8}''$ dia. on the $\frac{5}{8}''$ round.
     $\frac{13}{16}''$ dia. on $\frac{3}{4}''$ round.

Start bending the **D** shackle over the anvil back, keeping both ends even and the holes in alignment.

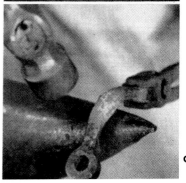

Complete the bend over a suitable size round bar or mandrel, and then line up the holes with a drift.

Note the extra metal surrounding the holes on the shackle in comparison with the trace hook.

The bow shackle is made in the same way. The ends are brought parallel and the holes aligned by driving a drift through with a spacer between. A large nut is placed between the anvil and the end of the shackle to prevent any distortion of the bow.

Here are the bow shackle; the shouldered pin and cotter made in Lessons 21 and 22; the hexagon-headed bolt made in Lesson 20; and the **D** shackle.

D

E

F

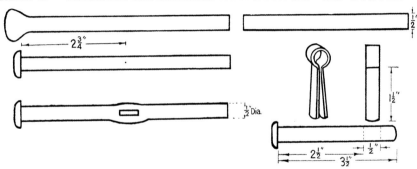

Take a NEAR WELDING heat on one end of a piece of ½" diameter bar 18" long, and upset one end as described in Lesson 13 A and B until the end is about twice the size of the bar.

Do not mark off for the slot until the head is formed.

Re-heat the upset end and lay it in the swage. Forge the head by striking at an angle of about 45°. Turn the bar a little between each blow to keep the head even.

Take a second heat and, keeping the head central on the bar, continue working it up until it is an even mushroom shape.

Keep the bar the original diameter, with a clean square shoulder underneath.

Now mark off and centre punch the slot.

To punch the slot, take a NEAR WELD-ING heat over the mark, lay the bar in the swage and, with the end of the slot punch on the dot, make a slot as in Lesson 16.

Dip the end of the punch in water, replace it in the hole and then forge in the swelling as much as possible to save the labour of filing it to size later.

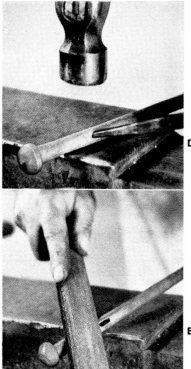

At a BRIGHT RED heat finish shaping to size and clean up any roughness with a bastard file.

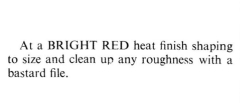

A 4″ length of ½″ × 16 s.w.g. is needed for the cotter.

It is made by folding the strip over a piece of ¼″ round then squeezing to shape between the vice jaws.

This is the finished cotter and pin for the shackle with turned eyes made in Lesson 17.

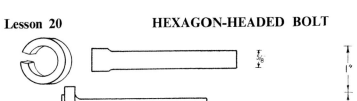

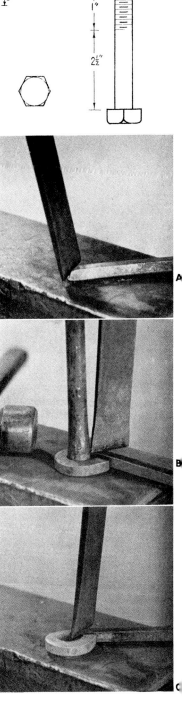

First upset one end of the ⅝″ round bar to a diameter of about ¾″.

The head of the bolt is made by welding on a collar made from ⅜″ square. This is a tricky weld, so it is better to use wrought iron for the collar as this gets hot quicker than the bolt. (Wrought iron, remember, will stand a higher temperature than mild steel).

Next, cut the end of the ⅜″ square to an angle of 45° so—

Hold the square bar over the tip of the bick with the point upwards and bend it into a tight circle. The metal will stretch while this is being done bringing the oblique end about square with the side of the bar.

Fit the collar over the upset end of the round bar and after allowing for a gap equal to the width of square metal, make a chisel mark like this—

Take a BRIGHT RED heat, cut off the bar at the chisel mark and fit the collar over the upset end of the ⅝″ bar.

Close the collar tightly around the bar and return to the fire.

Take a FULL WELDING heat very slowly so that the heat penetrates to the centre of the bar without burning the collar.

D

The ends of the collar must join at one corner of the hexagon. To close the ends and at the same time form the hexagon, *the order of the first three blows is most important.* Strike the first blow a little back from one end of the collar. This will partly close the gap. Before each of the next two blows, give the bar one-sixth of a turn. This will close the gap and the hexagon will form automatically between the hammer and the anvil. To complete the welding take a further heat. All subsequent blows must be delivered on the flats of the hexagon.

E

Before cleaning up the body of the bolt, true up the hexagon on the anvil face. Then lay the shank in the swage, and true up the diameter. Keep the head central and at right angles to the shank.

F

On all bolts the thickness of the collar should be half the diameter of the bolt or a little more according to the sizes of metal available.

In each case, the gap left is equal to the width of the square metal used for the collar.

G

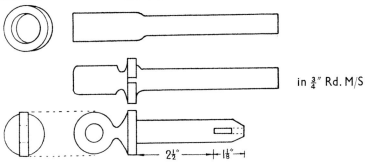

in $\frac{3}{4}''$ Rd. M/S

The shoulder under the eye of this shackle pin is formed by welding on a collar made as in Lesson 20.

Take a NEAR WELDING heat on one end of a $\frac{3}{4}''$ bar 18" long and make an upset 2" long. Weld on the collar at the base of the upset.

While still hot, fuller a groove all round like this—

Take a NEAR WELDING heat, flatten the end, shape roughly on the rounded edge of the anvil, then punch the hole.

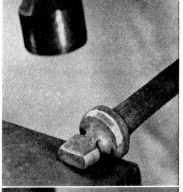

Take a fresh heat and work up the eye to shape with the point of the bick through the hole like this.

Complete the pin by slot punching the hole so that it is $\frac{5}{8}'' \times \frac{3}{16}''$, and cut off to length.

The finished pin is shown in Lesson 22 C.

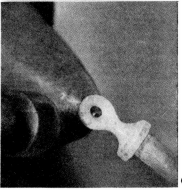

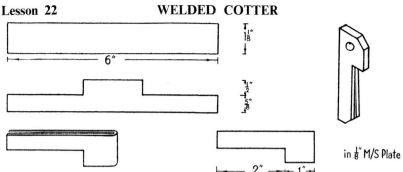

in $\frac{1}{8}''$ M/S Plate

Mark off a piece of $\frac{1}{8}''$ plate to the sizes given in the drawing. Using a cold chisel, cut the piece to the correct shape in the vice.

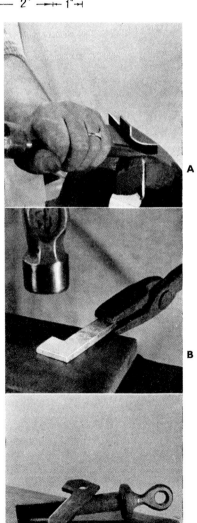

A

Take a BRIGHT RED heat and fold over flat. Then take a LIGHT WELDING heat on the head to about half way down and weld with light and rapid hammer blows without thinning the metal unduly.

Punch the hole with a round punch while hot.

B

File the cotter to fit the slot in the pin.

This is the finished pin and cotter for the bow shackle made in Lesson 18.

C

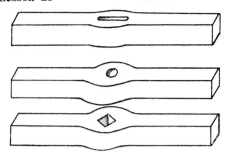
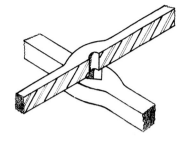

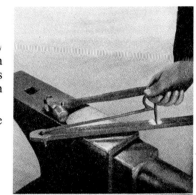

The position of the first hole in a harrow bar is marked with a centre punch. Each hole thereafter is marked from the previous one using the gauge or scriber made in Lesson 5.

Do not try to mark all the holes before starting to punch them.

The holes in *light* harrow frames are slotted and punched to the finished size and shape in one operation.

This is the special punch used for punching square holes in light harrow frames—

It combines the action of a slot punch with that of a square drift.

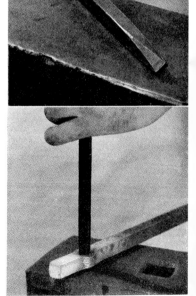

Do not attempt to punch the hole right through from one side, but use the punch as described in Lesson 16. As there is no upset, make sure that the slot is started exactly in the middle of the bar. It is important to keep as much metal as possible either side of the hole.

Round holes in light bars are made with a combined punch, similar to that shown in B on the opposite page, but it is of round instead of square section, like this—

Heavy flat bars are first slot-punched and then the hole is opened out by upsetting. This is being done here to the lower hole which is hot. The upper one is complete.

The hole is finished off with a special stubby drift, which is marked at three-quarters of the thickness of bar. It is driven in from each side in turn almost as far as the mark. This is done on the flat of the anvil and not over a hole. The use of the special drift prevents burrs forming on either edge of the hole.

Harrow tines must be a push fit in the holes. The holes must be spaced exactly so that the harrow frame can be assembled correctly. It is therefore essential to use a scriber to mark off each hole as the previous one is punched.

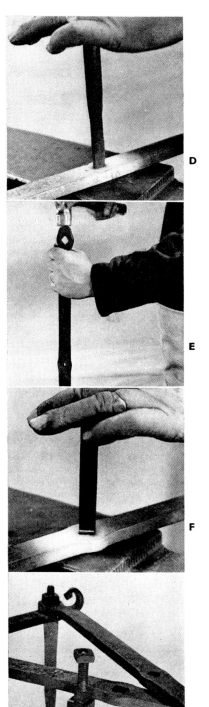

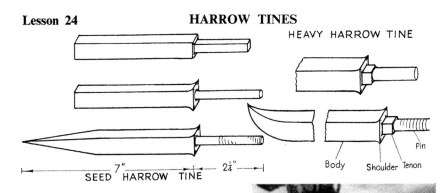

HEAVY HARROW TINE

Pin

Body   Shoulder   Tenon

SEED HARROW TINE

7"

2¼"

A shoulder on a seed harrow tine has a parallel round shank without a square tenon. Only a very slight reduction in section is needed to form a shoulder. Neither fullering nor swaging is necessary as the drawing down can be done by hammering the bar on the flat of the anvil and using the rounded edge of the anvil to form the shoulder.

Next drive the reduced portion of the tine into the countersunk side of the small round hole in the bolster. Withdraw the tine, reverse the bolster so that the square edged holes are uppermost, and drive the tine into the same hole. This completes the shoulder and forms the upset.

The special bolster used for forming the shoulders on tines is described in Chapter 2 and shown in Figs. 24 and 25 on pages 13 and 14.

This is the seed harrow tine as forged. The rounded pin, which will be threaded, continues right up to the shoulder without a square tenon.

Medium and heavy tines have a square tenon between the shoulder and the threaded portion. More reduction is required on these tines and the drawing down should be started over the bick of the anvil and completed on the flat, leaving both the tenon and the pin square.

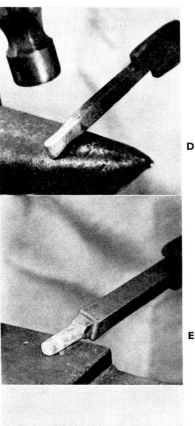

D

To square and upset the shoulder take a NEAR WELDING heat and drive the tine into the square hole in the bolster.

The pin, which is to be threaded, must now be rounded on the face of the anvil to the required size. It is then driven into the special round hole in the bolster; this will form the shoulder between the pin and the tenon and leave the tenon the required length.

E

Here a medium harrow tine is shown in three stages:
 (1) cut and marked,
 (2) the pin and tenon formed,
 (3) the tine pointed and set.

The square upset shoulder between the tine and the tenon, and the reduced shoulder between the tenon and the pin can be clearly seen.

F

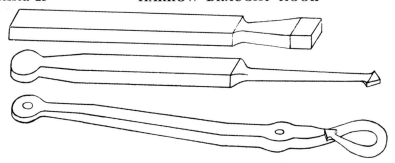

Approximately 18″ of $1\frac{1}{8}″ \times \frac{1}{2}″$ bar is used for the harrow draught hook.

Bring one end, which will form the hook, to a NEAR WELDING heat. Drawing down should be started on the anvil bick and finished off on the anvil face. The diamond head is formed as described in Lesson 16.

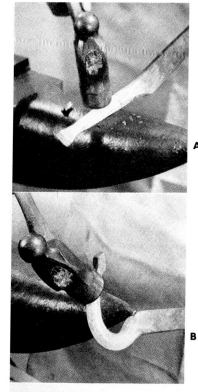

In forming the hook, the first bend is made on the top of the anvil bick as shown in Lesson 2. A harrow needs one right-handed and one left-handed hook. So, at the second stage of bending shown here, the point of one hook is turned to right and the point of the other hook to the left of the bar.

One completed hook for a diamond harrow frame should look like this—

The other should have the hook bent in the opposite direction, as shown in the drawing.

PART IV

PART IV

The lessons which follow are on more advanced forging and welding, calling for a higher degree of skill. By applying the techniques he has already learned, the knowledge gained by experience and by using common sense the student should have no difficulty in following the exercises.

BENDS TO DIMENSIONS

In making bends to measurements, allowance has to be made for the amount of metal used in actually forming the bend. The allowance will vary with the type of bend and with the individual smith; no hard and fast rule can be laid down. Experience will show what allowance to make, but the figures given below are a good guide for a start.

(a) Radius Bends

Radius bends should have the *inside* radius equal to the thickness of the metal. No preliminary upsetting is required.

To make the U-shaped piece from $1\frac{1}{4}'' \times \frac{1}{2}''$ shown in Lesson 26, subtract once the thickness of the metal for each bend from $3''$ which is the outside measurement over the bends. The marks will therefore be $2''$ apart.

If the two dots are kept in the middle of each bend and the correct radii maintained, the dots will finish up in line with the inside surfaces and the given measurement will be correct.

The same allowances are made for the Z bend in $1''$ round, also shown in Lesson 26, and again, if the correct inside radii are maintained the dots will finish up in line with the inside edge of each leg.

(b) Plain Square Corner Bends

Plain square corner bends have the inside corner forged square and the outside corner left rounded, and no *preliminary* upsetting is required. With light section, square and flat metal the corner can be strengthened by upsetting the material as the bend is made. The inner and outer corners must be forged simultaneously; if the inner one is squared first, it will be galled in forming the outer one.

To make the Z-shaped piece in $\frac{1}{2}''$ square shown in Lesson 28, *subtract* from the outside measurement half the thickness of the metal for each bend. If the dots are kept on the diagonal line joining the inner and outer corners of each bend, the finished measurement will be correct.

Although the shape is different, the same allowances are made for bending both the shaft staple in Lesson 27 and the U-bolt in Lesson 28. Again, the dots should be kept on the diagonal line through the corners of each bend.

(c) Forged Square Corner Bends

Forged square corner bends are upset before bending starts. The extra metal is then worked into the bend to form a corner square on the outside and with a radius on the inside.

To make the **Z**-shaped piece in Lesson 29 (which has a square corner on the outside and the radius on the inside of each bend) it is first necessary to upset the metal to $1\frac{1}{2}$ times its thickness where each bend will be formed. To the outside measurement, add a quarter of the thickness of the material and mark the bar. Next, upset the bar evenly around the mark using $1\frac{1}{2}$ times the thickness of the material for each upset. The overall length of the bar will now be reduced by three times its thickness. The marks will be $1\frac{1}{4}$ times the thickness of the bar closer together than the outside measurement of the finished bend. If the marks are now kept on a diagonal line through the corner, the outside measurement will again be correct.

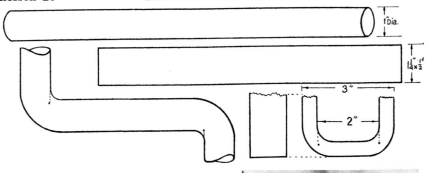

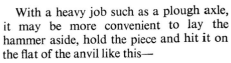

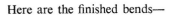

Mark off as described on page 78, paragraph (*a*).

Take a NEAR WELDING heat, adjust the position of the heat if necessary by cooling out with water (Lesson 15, B and C) and bend over the bick. The second bend is made in the same way.

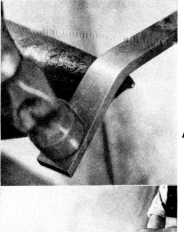

With a heavy job such as a plough axle, it may be more convenient to lay the hammer aside, hold the piece and hit it on the flat of the anvil like this—

The weight of the metal itself will then do the bending.

Here are the finished bends—

In the smaller one the punch marks can be seen in the middle of each bend.

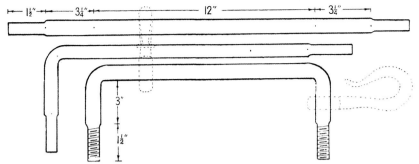

Mark off a $\frac{1}{2}''$ round bar as shown in the drawing, using the allowances described on page 78, paragraph (b).

Take a NEAR WELDING heat, and from the mark nearest one end, reduce the diameter to $\frac{7}{16}''$. There is no need to use a bottom swage for this operation: square it with a hammer, then round up as described in Lesson 1.

Test the diameter in a $\frac{7}{16}''$ hole.

A

Next, take a BRIGHT RED heat at the second mark and, keeping the mark on one side bend the bar over the bick of the anvil.

B

Take a NEAR WELDING heat in the bend, with the long part lying in a bottom swage and the short end upwards, and strike the top with a hammer to drive the bend into the swage. This will upset the metal slightly and produce a sharp bend, with the punch mark exactly in the middle of the side of the thickened corner.

Reduce and bend the other end in the same way; then twist out of alignment for threading as described for the U-bolt in Lesson 2. Twist straight again.

C

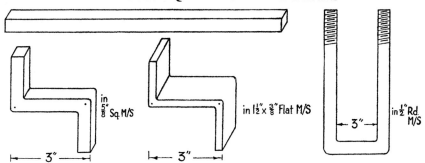

in $\frac{5}{8}''$ Sq. M/S

in $1\frac{1}{2}'' \times \frac{3}{8}''$ Flat M/S

in $\frac{1}{2}''$ Rd. M/S

To make the **Z** or cranked bends, mark the $\frac{5}{8}''$ square and $1\frac{1}{2}'' \times \frac{3}{8}''$ flat as described on page 78, paragraph (*b*) allowing half the thickness of the metal for each bend.

At a NEAR WELDING heat bend the bar over the rounded edge of anvil with the mark on the side of the bar beyond the edge of the anvil, as shown here—

Take another heat, cool out the end and square the corner by laying the long part of the bar on the anvil face and striking the short end, so—

This will upset the metal slightly and produce a sharp bend with the punch mark exactly in the middle of the side of the thickened corner.

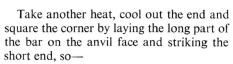

Keep the metal from thickening by flattening the swelling on the side of the corner as you go.

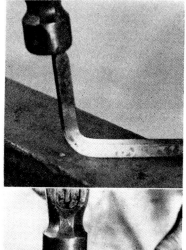

Finish off by gripping in the vice with the inside corner about $\frac{3}{16}''$ from the vice jaws and finally square the bend by hammering like this—

Do not drive the inside corner hard against the jaws or the sharp edge will cut it.

Make the other bend in the same way.

D

To make the U-bolt, mark off the $\frac{1}{2}''$ round, using the same allowances.

Take a NEAR WELDING heat where the bar will be bent, quench to about $\frac{3}{4}''$ on either side of the punch mark and bend with a full radius over the anvil bick.

E

Lay it in a bottom swage and work up the corner like this—

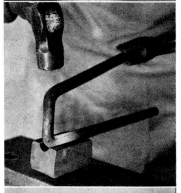

F

In order to screw the ends, bend one side as shown to allow the die-stock to rotate.

G

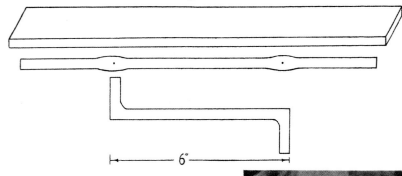

Mark a $1\frac{1}{4}'' \times \frac{1}{2}''$ bar using the allowances given on page 78, paragraph (c).

Take a NEAR WELDING heat, keeping the punch mark exactly in the middle of the heat.

Cool out leaving $\frac{3}{4}''$ hot on either side of the mark.

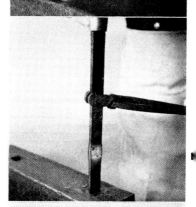

Next, upset the bar evenly each side of the mark until the overall length of the bar is reduced by exactly $1\frac{1}{2}$ times the thickness of the metal.

Two or more heats are required to produce this amount of upset and its shape and position can be controlled by suitable quenching.

Repeat the upsetting around the second mark, again reducing the overall length of the bar by $1\frac{1}{2}$ times its thickness, so that the total reduction is now three times the thickness.

Here is the bar upset—

Note the evenness of the swellings.

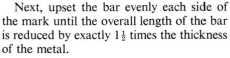

Bend over the anvil bick to form the inside radius. This radius should never be allowed to become too small.

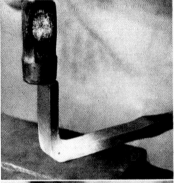

Start to work up the bend, as shown here, keeping the punch mark on the diagonal of the corner.

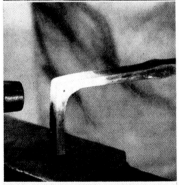

Continue working up the bend like this, keeping a full inside radius and finishing the outside corner to a sharp square edge.

Here is the finished piece—

Note the large amount of metal which has been worked into the bends, the sharp outside corners and the perfectly smooth flowing radius on the inside of each bend.

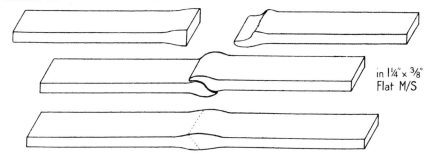

in 1¼" × ⅜"
Flat M/S

Before starting these welding lessons, study carefully the description of fire welding in Chapter 4, page 21.

Take a NEAR WELDING heat on each bar in turn and upset the ends which are to be welded to ½" thick, but keep the width the same.

Before starting a large scarf, the upset end of the bar should be forged to a short bevel, leaving the edge about $\frac{3}{16}$" thick like this—

The hammer blows should be delivered at an angle of 45°.

Next, with the bevelled edge downwards over the rounded edge of the anvil, forge the scarf as shown here—

Before starting to weld, remove any clinker from the fire which must be clean with a good heart.

Lay both pieces side by side in the fire with the scarf lips on top. To ensure they are both heating equally, jockey them about and, as they approach welding heat, draw each in turn to the edge of the fire to judge the heat. If sand is being used as a flux now is the time to sprinkle a little on each piece.

Now work quickly—take both pieces from the fire together, tap them over the edge of the anvil to knock off the dirt, and lay them on the anvil with the scarfs matching and the middles in contact.

The order of the first three blows is important:

First on the centre of the top scarf so that any dirt is driven out towards the ends.

Second on the thick part of the top scarf so that it welds to the thin end of the under scarf which is being chilled by the anvil face.

Third on the thin end of the top scarf before this cools.

If another heat is necessary to complete the weld, take it now.

Continue welding by turning the piece to and fro, hammering both sides alternately. Take care not to reduce the section below the size of the original bar.

The completed weld should be like this, with no reduction of section and with the corners very slightly chamfered.

The finish of the weld should be smooth, as a rough edge or a hammer mark may cause a fracture to start.

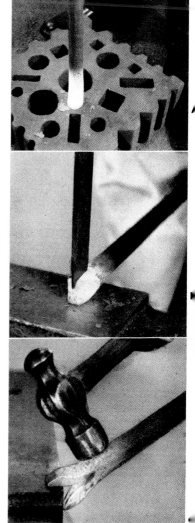

Take a NEAR WELDING heat on the end of one bar and upset to about $1\frac{1}{4}$ times the original size. This can be done by tamping as shown here—

Place the upset end on the anvil face and, holding it at an angle, forge to a blunt chisel end leaving the edge $\frac{5}{16}$ " thick.

Take a fresh heat and split this end by cutting into each side in turn with the hot chisel.

Force the ends apart as far as possible with the chisel.

Take a fresh heat and open out the cleft end over the edge of the anvil to a little less than a right angle. Then lay it on one side of the fire to retain the heat while the other piece is being prepared.

Lesson 31—*cont.*

Take a NEAR WELDING heat on the second bar and upset the end a little less than the first bar.

Forge to an abrupt chisel end which fits into the cleft and then close tightly together at a BRIGHT RED heat, like this—

The weld can be made in two ways.

D

First method. No assistant available

If no help is available, heat the two pieces side by side as described in Lesson 30.

Take a FULL WELDING heat and drop one piece into a suitable hole in the swage-block with the cleft end uppermost. Place the wedge end in the cleft and drive down hard with a couple of quick hammer blows.

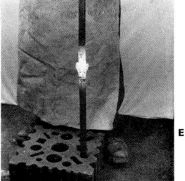

E

Replace the partly-welded bar in the fire, take a fresh welding heat and continue welding by jumping the bar vertically on the swage-block like this—

Weld in the lips on the anvil face and then finish off with a hand hammer in a bottom swage.

F

Second method. With assistance

If help is available, set the two pieces together as shown in D above and place them carefully in the heart of the fire without disturbing the set-up.

Take a FULL WELDING heat and, without removing the bar from the fire, drive the cleft into the weld until it feels solid while your assistant holds a sledge hammer or heavy weight against the other end of the bar. Lift out of the fire immediately and weld in the lips of the cleft, finishing off between swages.

G

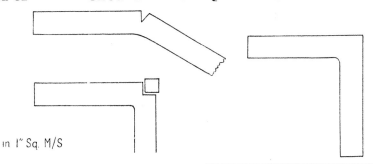

in 1" Sq. M/S

Mark off where the centre of the bend is required.

Take a NEAR WELDING heat and with the hot chisel on the mark, make a cut nearly halfway through the bar.

Bend the bar over bick to a right angle keeping a good radius on the inside like this—

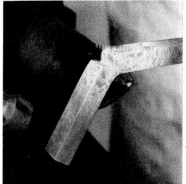

The inset is made from a bar of the same thickness and should be about $\frac{1}{4}''$ longer than the width of the metal from which the bend is made.

Cut into both sides with a hot chisel and leaving just enough in the middle to support the end when it is being tacked into place.

Take a LIGHT WELDING heat on both pieces and tack the inset into place with the bend over the bick like this (shown cold)—

When securely in place break the inset of the bar off at the notches and dress the cut face so that it looks like this (shown cold)—

Take a FULL WELDING heat and, to ensure that both sides of the inset are welded right into the corner, strike the first blow downwards on the top of the inset so—

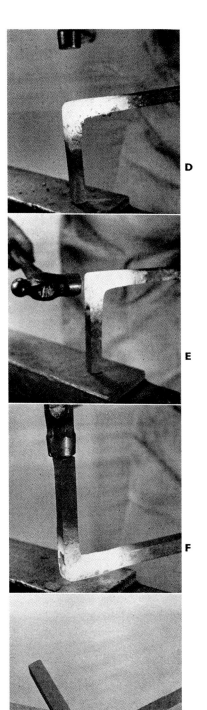

Immediately strike the second blow endways like this—

Continue with alternate blows until the weld is solid.

To keep the greatest strength in the bend, work up the corner on the anvil face, like this—

Do not place the inside of the corner over the edge of the anvil or the bick as this will reduce the section of the metal across the corner and so weaken the bend.

The completed bend should have a square outside corner and a good inside radius as shown here.

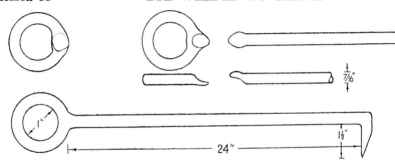

To make the shank cut off 26" from a ⅞" round with a cold chisel.

Bring one end to NEAR WELDING heat and start upsetting by tamping direct on the anvil as shown here—

or by hammer blows on the top with the rod standing upright on the anvil.

Straighten the resultant buckling.

Take another NEAR WELDING heat and finish upsetting by striking the hot end with a hammer like this—

Flatten the end a little and make a double wing-shaped scarf by working over the rounded edge of the anvil.

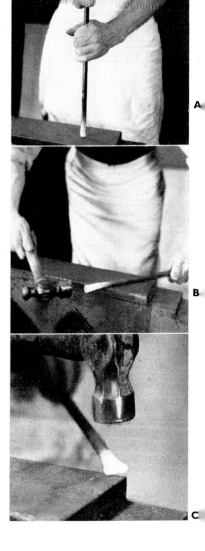

The finished scarf must have a good shoulder between the flattened part and the rod, and must be shaped like this—

Make the ring as described in Lesson 13 and while the welded portion is still hot, forge it into a scarf over the corner of the anvil, like this—

The ring made previously will do, but in this case, bring it to BRIGHT RED heat before making the scarf.

The set-up is here shown cold—

Take a FULL WELDING heat on both pieces together, lay the ring on the anvil with the flat of the scarf downwards. Immediately lay the shank on top with the scarfs matching and start to weld with light blows at first, striking harder as the metal unites.

While it is still hot, dress up the eye on the bick and then the shank on the anvil face with the shoulder of the eye over the rounded edge.

When finished, it should look like this—

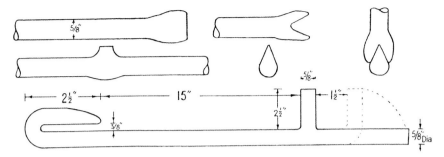

Mark off to suit the length of scroll wrench required.

Upset the part forming the top of the **T** around the mark. Then, using the peen of the hammer, forge a *one-sided* scarf, keeping the underlip flat on the anvil face like this—

Place it on the edge of the fire to retain the heat.

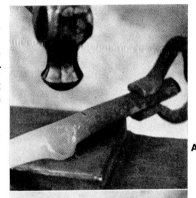

The leg of the **T** is made by first upsetting one end and then forging a double winged scarf.

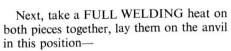

Next, take a FULL WELDING heat on both pieces together, lay them on the anvil in this position—

The first blow should be on the thick back of the top scarf so that it welds to the thin end of the under scarf before this is chilled by the anvil.

Continue by hammering towards the top of the **T**.

Dress up over the rounded edge of the anvil.

Lesson 34—*cont.*

Cleft Weld

The alternative method of welding a **T** is a little more difficult, but results in a much stronger joint.

Start by forging a *double-sided* scarf on the bar where the leg of the **T** is to be welded. Hammer on both sides and draw out the lip a little longer than in the other method.

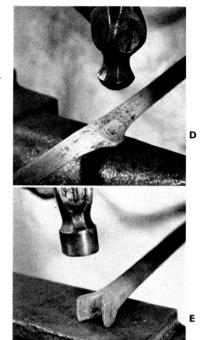
D

Next make a cleft end on the leg of the **T** by first upsetting and drawing to a blunt chisel end which is split as described in Lesson 31.

E

At a BRIGHT RED heat, set the two pieces together and hammer first on the top of the cleft bar and then on the lips to form a perfect fit.

Take a FULL WELDING heat on both pieces together, lay the long bar on the anvil and start welding by driving the cleft portion over the bottom scarf so that the root of the **V** of the weld takes first.

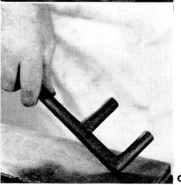
F

Take another FULL WELDING heat and weld in the lips of the scarfs.

The completed weld is shown here made into a scroll wrench; the end has been bent as in Lesson 27.

G

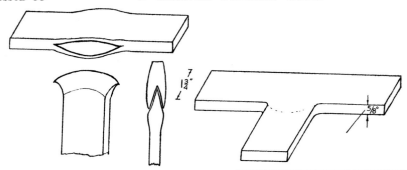

Take a NEAR WELDING heat on the middle of the piece which forms the top of the **T**. Upset to $1\frac{1}{2}$ times the thickness with extra metal on one edge of the bar to form a bulge like this—

Take a fresh heat and draw this side bulge into a lip with a blunt edge about $\frac{3}{16}''$ thick as shown here—

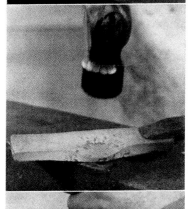

Take a NEAR WELDING heat and split this lip down the middle with a hot chisel to form a semi-circular pocket to receive the fan-shaped scarf on the piece which will be welded in.

Lay on the side of the fire to retain the heat while the next piece is being prepared.

Take a NEAR WELDING heat on the end of the piece which will form the leg of the **T** and upset it for about $\frac{1}{2}''$.

Forge the upset into a fan-shaped chisel end, drawing as much metal as possible to the sides, like this—

Take a BRIGHT RED heat and drive the chisel end hard down into the pocket, making sure that it reaches the bottom before closing in the lips, thus—

Lay both pieces side by side in the fire. To prevent burning the thin edges of the pocketed piece it must stand on edge with the lips upwards.

Take a FULL WELDING heat and start the weld by driving the long end right down to the bottom of the pocket.

Concentrate on getting the full width of the fan solidly welded into the bottom and ends of the pocket, leaving the lips till the next heat.

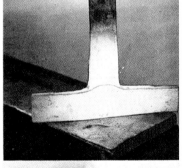

Take another FULL WELDING heat and complete the weld by closing in the lips, leaving a small radius in the corners of the **T**.

97

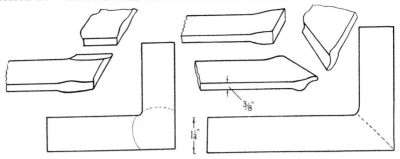

Diagonal Scarf Weld

The quickest way to weld a square corner is to use diagonal scarfs, but the resulting joint is not so strong as the straight scarf method.

Take a NEAR WELDING heat on each piece in turn and after upsetting the ends cut them off at an angle of 45°, leaving a blunt corner, like this—

Take another heat and, using the rounded edge of the anvil, forge a scarf on the same side of each piece, so that they pair up when laid on top of each other at a right angle with the scarfs matching as shown in the next illustration.

Take a FULL WELDING heat on both pieces together and lay them on the anvil as shown.

Strike the first blow on the thick part of the top scarf so that it welds to the thin part of the under scarf which is being chilled by the anvil face.

Finish off with a minimum of blows so as not to reduce the thickness, because a diagonal scarf has no surplus metal in the finished weld.

Straight Scarf Weld

A straight scarf corner weld has greater strength than a diagonal scarf weld, but it takes longer to prepare and make.

Take a NEAR WELDING heat on each piece in turn and upset, first quenching the tip so that the swelling starts about $\frac{3}{4}''$ from the end.

After upsetting take another heat and form a scarf on the edge of one side of the bar from the end to the middle of the upset.

D

Each bar is scarfed on the same side so that when one piece is turned over and laid under the other at right angles as shown here, the side scarf on each piece must be in contact with the upset part of the other piece.

E

Take a FULL WELDING heat and deliver the first blow on the thick part of the top piece to weld the thin under scarf before it is chilled by the anvil face. Continue hammering across the thin part of the top scarf making sure that the inside corner is welded at this heat.

Take another FULL WELDING heat and finish by hammering from the inside to the outside of the corner.

F

There is no need to forge in the superfluous metal, so trim it off with a hot chisel; ample has been allowed for the strength of the joint.

The finished welds should look like this with no reduction in section, and a small radius on the inside corner.

G

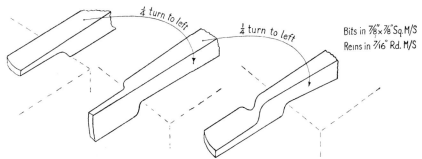

Bits in ⅞″×⅞″ Sq. M/S
Reins in ⁷⁄₁₆″ Rd. M/S

To forge a pair of tongs, cut off a piece 12″ long from a ⅞″ square bar.

Take a LIGHT WELDING heat and, with the end over the rounded edge of the anvil like this, forge a shoulder, leaving the end ⅜″ thick × 1¾″ long × 1″ wide.

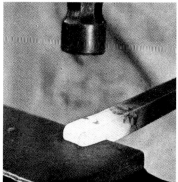

There should be a good radius at the base of the shoulder and the end should look like this—

Take another LIGHT WELDING heat and from the position shown in A above give the bar a quarter turn to the *left* and place it over the rounded edge of the far side of the anvil. Move the left hand slightly to the *left* and forge a second shoulder to form a boss.

The end should now look like this—

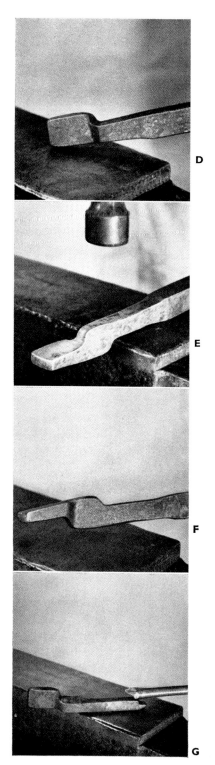

D

Take another LIGHT WELDING heat and, from the position shown in C, give the bar another quarter turn to the *left* and, again using the far edge of the anvil, forge a third shoulder.

The bar behind the boss is reduced to a $\frac{5}{8}''$ square section.

The completed jaw is shown here—

E

The second jaw is made on the other end of the bar in exactly the same way. Remember to turn the bar to the *left* each time. The two finished jaws are alike, not opposites.

F

Cut the jaws apart and scarf the cut ends of the reduced square sections. Weld a piece of $\frac{7}{16}''$ round to each jaw to form the reins.

G

To retain the maximum strength in the boss the rivet holes should be punched, not drilled. Start to punch as shown with the shoulder downwards over the edge of the anvil.

Turn over on to the flat side and complete punching over the anvil hole.

The method of making a rivet for a pair of tongs is described on the next page.

The tong jaws and the rivet are put together cold and all made hot together before riveting up.

After the rivet is clenched and while the jaws are still hot, they should be set to the size of material it is intended to hold. The spacing of the reins should be adjusted at the same time, so that they are comfortable to grip.

Dip the tongs in the water trough, opening and closing them as they cool to ease them.

Rivet for Tongs

The rivet is made from ⅜″ round metal, the shank being reduced between top and bottom swages like this—

M

Cut off as shown, allowing sufficient length of the full-size section to form the head.

N

The head is then formed by setting the piece down in bolster, thus—

and is worked up either on the anvil face or by using a rivet snap.

O

RECOMMENDED FURTHER READING

Hints on Steel, *by Lord Riverdale*

Arthur Balfour & Co. Ltd, Capital Steel Works, Sheffield.

Fowler's Mechanics' and Machinists' Pocket Book

Scientific Publishing Co., 316, Manchester Road, Timperley, Manchester.

Blacksmith's Manual Illustrated, *by J. W. Lillico*

Technical Press, Ltd, Gloucester Road, Kingston Hill, Surrey.

Iron and Steel Today, *by J. Dearden*

Oxford University Press, Amen House, Warwick Square, London, E.C.4.

The Value of Science in the Smithy and Forge, *by W. H. Cathcart* (4th Edition)

Charles Griffen & Co. Ltd, 42, Drury Lane, London, W.C.2.

Tables for the Use of Blacksmiths and Forgers, *by John Watson*

Longmans Green & Co. Ltd, 6 & 7, Clifford Street, London, W.1.

Practical Farriery, *by C. Richardson*

Sir Isaac Pitman & Son Ltd, Parker Street, London, W.C.1.

Practical Smithing and Forging, *by Thomas Moore* (out of print)

E. & F. N. Spon, Ltd, 15, Bedford Street, London, W.C.2.

The Structure of Steel Simply Explained, *by Eric Simons and Edwin Gregory*

Blackie & Son, Ltd, 17, Stanhope Street, Glasgow.

Steel Manufacture Simply Explained, *by Eric Simons and Edwin Gregory*

Sir Isaac Pitman & Sons Ltd, Parker Street, London, W.C.1.

Hardening and Tempering Steel, *by Bernard E. Jones* (out of print)

Cassell & Co. Ltd, 37-38, St. Andrews Hill, Queen Victoria Street, London, E.C.4.

Machinery's Screw Thread Book

Machinery Publishing Co. Ltd, National House, West Street, Brighton, 1.

Iron and Steel Catalogue

Dunlop & Ranken Ltd, 147, The Head Bow, Leeds.

Chart 13. Thickness of Blanks Required for Making Hammered Forgings

Machinery Publishing Co. Ltd, National House, West Street, Brighton, 1.

Chart 30. Showing Weight in lbs. per foot of Round, Square, Hexagon and Flat Steel Bars

Machinery Publishing Co. Ltd, Nation House, West Street, Brighton, 1.